Jeff Apter has been writing professionally for more than fifteen years, having spent five years as music editor at Australian *Rolling Stone*. His work has been published in the *Sydney Morning Herald*, the *West Australian*, *Juice* and various other newspapers, magazines and websites, and his insightful views on popular culture have been aired on MTV, ABC Newcastle, Triple J and numerous other radio and TV programs. He is currently a contributing editor to *GQ* magazine and writes for both *The Bulletin* and *Vogue*. His first book was the 2003 Silverchair biography *Tomorrow Never Knows*; *Fornication: The Red Hot Chili Peppers Story* followed in July 2004. Jeff lives in Sydney with his wife Diana and baby daughter Elizabeth Asha, and proudly recalls how he once topped the batting averages for the Revesby Workers U-16s.

SLATS

The Michael Slater Story

Michael Slater

with Jeff Apter

Foreword by Mark Taylor

RANDOM HOUSE AUSTRALIA

Random House Australia Pty Ltd
20 Alfred Street, Milsons Point, NSW 2061
http://www.randomhouse.com.au

Sydney   New York   Toronto
London   Auckland   Johannesburg

First published by Random House Australia 2005

National Library of Australia
Cataloguing-in-Publication Entry:

Slater, Michael, 1970–.
Slats: the Michael Slater story.

ISBN 1 74051 378 9

1. Slater, Michael, 1970–. 2. Cricket players – Australia
– Biography. 3. Cricket – Australia. I. Apter, Jeff, 1961–.
II. Title.

796.358092

Cover illustration by Newspix
Cover design by Darian Causby/Highway 51 Design Works
Typesetting and internal design by Midland Typesetters, Maryborough, Victoria
Printed and bound by Griffin Press, Netley, South Australia

10 9 8 7 6 5 4 3 2 1

*I dedicate this book to my loving and supportive family.
In particular, Mum and Dad for encouraging me as a
youngster and beyond to chase my cricketing dream.*

Contents

Acknowledgments

Firstly, to my dad, Peter, and brothers, Julian and Mark – thanks for the many torrid backyard cricket tussles over the years. I fully realise now how important this was in my development as a young cricketer (and I apologise for being just a little too competitive at times).

Words just can't express how influential Warren Smith was, not just in my career, but life also. From when I was seven years old, he quickly passed on to me a love and passion for the game that still burns brightly today. He has also been like a second father to me, and his support after Mum left will never be forgotten. To my number one coach and friend, thank you so much.

I'd also like to mention Clive Robertson, who organised an opportunity for me and other talented young cricketers to play for Balmain in the Green Shield competition in Sydney during the mid 1980s. This was a crucial stepping stone and gave me important exposure in the big smoke.

To all the selectors, coaches, managers and team-mates over the years – I appreciate your belief in me and, above all, your camaraderie and special memories. It was a lot of fun.

As you will read, at times my health hasn't been the best. Two men deserve a special mention: Patrick Farhart

(NSW physiotherapist) and Ken Crichton (North Sydney Sports Medical Centre) were a huge reason why I was able to function out on the pitch. In desperate moments they worked tirelessly to help get my arthritis under control. Full credit must go to them because until my final retirement, I had never missed a game of cricket because of this debilitating disease. These men are both legends and I feel blessed to have been able to trust such talented professionals with my health.

Stephanie Slater (née Blackett) was my childhood sweetheart and partner for most of my career. Her friendship and support will always remain a very special part of my life. Thanks Steph.

I always wanted to write a book at the conclusion of my career, but knew the timing had to be right. I was only going to commit to this project when I felt I could give an honest reflection on some pretty difficult periods of my life. Thanks to Mark Ray for the early groundwork and story development he did.

And to Jeff Apter, one of Australia's prominent music journalists. He wasn't the obvious choice to take on this book, but a cricket tragic at heart (and former right-arm firebrand). Jeff's enthusiasm, dedication and day-to-day professionalism made this book what it is. Thanks also to his wife, Diana, who helped with the proofreading whilst pregnant with their daughter, Elizabeth.

I've been travelling around the globe while this book has been in production and Random House have been fantastic to work with – I appreciate this opportunity in telling my life story to date.

Acknowledgments

And finally, to my fiancée, Jo. I have always believed there is no coincidence in life. Therefore I know that the fateful night we met was always meant to happen. You are the most amazing human being I have ever met, Jo, and I look forward to the rest of our lives together.

Michael Slater
Bridgetown, Barbados
May 2005

Foreword
by Mark Taylor

My first recollection of Michael Slater was in the suburbs of Wagga Wagga as an eight-year-old boy, who persisted in annoying me and his elder brother Julian, whom I'd played cricket with for a number of years. Julian was the captain of the Lake Albert Under-14s, which I was also a member of, and we would often get together for a 'hit' in the streets outside his house. Michael was a pest, always hanging around looking to join in, and as you can imagine, an eight-year-old is certainly not welcome in a game of cricket involving teenage boys. I can't tell you what he was like in those days as I, like all the older boys, tried to ignore him in the hope that he would go away. What I can tell you is that we weren't terribly successful in getting rid of him!

It wasn't till the early 1990s, when I had found my way into the Australian cricket team and Slats was a young man on the verge of first-class cricket, that I realised he'd been quite right in hanging around with the older boys playing cricket. He had and still has a great passion for the game of cricket, but more importantly he had a wonderful technique as a batsman which I'm sure was honed in the back streets of Wagga, belting the older and more experienced boys around. I learned this from watching him in the nets at the Adelaide Oval, where he was stationed with the Cricket Academy. From just one net session you could see that he possessed a keen eye for the ball and exhibited a great range in his footwork: going well forward to drive the ball but also getting well back on his stumps to play the hook, pull and cut shots.

His only weakness lay in the field, where he was extremely fast across the turf but lacked the softness of hand with his catching. I can recall Slats badgering me many times during his career to try him out in the slips. I eventually relented in 1998 in a tour match against a provincial side in Karachi, Pakistan.

Michael was tired of fielding in the covers that hot day and wanted to show me what he could do. He lasted approximately five overs and dropped two catches, both off the bowling of Stuart Magill, who was becoming increasingly agitated. After the first dropped catch (which wasn't all that easy, to be fair), Michael came to me and suggested that I go back into slip. I told him that a good slipper must ride out the days he drops a catch or two and hang in there. After the second dropped catch, which was an absolute sitter, Slats pleaded with me to take him out of there only moments before Stuart Magill was demanding his removal. Needless to say, Slats never returned to the slip cordon.

There was rarely a dull moment opening the batting with Slats. Being an extremely aggressive but nervous opener, he often played many expansive shots at the start of his innings. This led to either exciting viewing for the fans or to a very jumpy number three batsman sitting in the changerooms, expecting to be walking out to bat after every ball that Michael faced. This approach, however, won many games for Australia and rocked many opening bowlers. None more so than Phillip DeFreitas, the English opening bowler who Slats took apart at the start of the Ashes Series in Australia in 1994/95. This was my first home series as a captain so I was a little nervous. Batting first at the Gabba in Brisbane can be a little nerve-racking, but after Slats belted consecutive fours off the first two balls from DeFrietas – one through the covers and one through point – the Poms were on the back foot from that moment on. He finished with 176 that day and was out half an hour before stumps, and I believe that innings went a long way towards retaining the Ashes for Australia.

That day at the Gabba, I was run out. There is no doubt that Slats was much quicker between the wickets than me, but I was having a lot of trouble with his calling. It took me another couple of near run-outs to work out Michael's 'unusual' calling technique. I mentioned that he was a nervous starter as a batsman, well, he was also a very excitable player, particularly when he'd hit a good shot. As soon as he'd hit the ball well, he would always call 'Yes' very loudly, irrespective of where the ball had gone. As you can imagine, if the ball went straight to a fielder, the odds of a run-out were good, particularly if I responded to the call. Eventually I deduced that when it came to running between the wickets with Slats you had to respond not to what he said but the *volume* of the words he spoke. A loud, excited call of 'YES' would simply mean, *Yes, I've hit the ball well*. It was the second, calmer call of 'No', after the ball had gone straight to the field, that I needed to wait for. By the end of my career I had figured out his calling technique, which was a real advantage that we had as a combination. The fielding side were often mystified as to why a loud call of 'Yes' would see me heading back into my crease.

Slats and I struck up a good opening combination during the 1990s and it was one that I particularly enjoyed. We are certainly very different characters but we both enjoyed the fact that we were different and never compared to each other. He was a dashing right-hander and I was the more subdued left-hander. Standing at the non-striker's end watching Slats in full flight, taking to the bowlers, was certainly a pleasure I won't forget. He was the type of player who would at times disappoint himself and his admirers because his aggressive approach would lead to his downfall. He was sometimes criticised for being rash or irresponsible. I believe that cricket is a much more enjoyable game to play and watch when people like Michael Slater are playing it. Much like Michael Clarke these days, they are the type of batsmen who bring the fans through the gates and get people to switch on their TVs to watch. They are also the ones who win games for their teams or change the outcome of matches in a short period of time. The game is much richer from their presence.

Michael, as you will read, can be a complex individual. However, on the cricket field he was quite simple. He loved playing and loved attacking, which was an enormous benefit to the sides that I was lucky enough to be in alongside him. I'm sure that you'll enjoy reading about my opening partner in *SLATS* ...

Introduction

Walk This Way

I've taken a lot of different walks in my cricketing career. They've ranged from the jubilant victory lap of a player who has just helped to win the Ashes for Australia, to the slow, sad trudge off the oval after scoring a duck; from the hot, sweaty struggle across the paddock between overs as the Australian sun belts down on you, to the unnerving 'dead man walking' sensation of heading to the captain's room knowing that you're about to be dropped. There was even a time during my days at the Australian Cricket Academy when I couldn't walk at all, after I'd been knocked off my bike by a car. But there is no stranger walk in all of cricket than the one that takes you from the Lord's dressing room onto the ground of Lord's itself, the sacred home of cricket in St John's Wood, London.

Lord's is deeply layered with history. The ground is so steeped in the legends and traditions of the game I love and

1

played at the highest level that you can almost smell the history there. Yet despite the ground's rich glories, I remember my first walk at Lord's for a completely different reason: it was just so hard to get from the dressing sheds to the centre of play.

The first time I took that journey was as opening batsman alongside Mark Taylor on 17 June 1993, as part of the champion Australian touring team of that year. It was an amazing, surreal moment. Despite the huge highs and deep lows I'd experienced in the 23 years leading up to that tour, my rise to the Australian team had been lightning fast: I'd only played twelve first-class matches when I was picked for the 1993 squad. In comparison, heroes of mine like Greg Chappell had played almost 100 games before getting the nod. So I knew I was very fortunate – even more so as my team-mate Matthew Hayden had been fancied as Mark Taylor's new opening partner, but I'd scored strongly in the games prior to the Tests and had been given this huge opportunity. I'd done well enough in the First Test at Old Trafford, which we'd won, to be able to strap on the pads that June morning alongside Taylor, the man known universally as 'Tubby'.

Leading up to the Lord's Test I was on such a high that I smashed the ball during our practice sessions, which was out of character because I usually treated net sessions as I would an innings: I'd watch the ball carefully early on and only go for my shots when I was fully set. But before Lord's I was unstoppable. Then there was all the off-field lead-up – the team meeting, the team dinner – which I soaked up like a sponge.

The night before the start of the Test match, however, was bizarre. Even though I was rooming with the very mellow batsman Mark Waugh, a man so laid-back and unobtrusive that you sometimes had to check that he was really there, I barely slept at all. I dozed for maybe a couple of hours, tops; most of the night I was playing my upcoming innings in my head. I didn't force myself to do this; I simply couldn't avoid it. All my thoughts were positive as I slipped into a sort of reverie in the middle of the night, a half-dream state where I played a technically perfect innings on the biggest cricketing stage of all. I saw myself playing the full array of shots, including lavish cover drives and big pulls. When the ball came down the pitch, I hit it spectacularly. Every shot was sweet and I never saw myself getting out. The images were so vivid that I didn't even try to sleep and spent the whole night in a semi-daze watching them.

I swear that when the alarm went off in the morning I'd already played my innings from beginning to end. This only happened one other time in my career, before playing New Zealand in the Third Test in Hobart during the 1993/94 Aussie summer. That experience was slightly different though: before the match against the Kiwis I had slept well, but I'd had a strong visualisation of my innings the morning before the match – and I scored 168.

On the morning of the Lord's Test I felt exhausted, but after having a shower, putting on my Australian tracksuit and going down for breakfast, I was energised again. I knew that whatever happened, it was going to be the most amazing experience I'd had in the game so far.

Before every Test, the captains of the two teams go onto the pitch where a coin is tossed to decide who will bat first. The captain who wins the toss chooses whether his team will bat or bowl first, depending on pitch and weather conditions. Our skipper Allan Border (AB) had lost every toss on that tour to date, so we'd never had the benefit of deciding whether to bat or bowl first. This time, however, he called correctly and won the toss. And despite there being a lot of moisture around – a sure-fire indication that the ball would swing, which would suit the bowling side – he decided that we'd bat first. From the moment I heard AB say, 'We're batting, boys.', this crazy mix of adrenaline and nerves surged through my body. Tubby and I didn't say much to each other. We just knew what we had to do: get through the new ball and get our side off to the right kind of start.

Now, I was never the kind of guy to be in my batting gear and ready to go early. Instead, I liked to fiddle around in the dressing room. Otherwise you end up sitting there in your batting gear with nothing to do but think about the innings to come, which would always bring on a serious bout of nerves. Usually someone would decide to get me moving and call out, 'Come on, Slats. You've got five minutes.' But at Lord's I was ready too early, and had far too much spare time on my hands. I was out of my normal routine: I had huge butterflies in my stomach and as I sat there with my gloves already on, I looked down and saw sweat starting to seep through the leather of my pads. I hadn't played a shot, I hadn't even left the dressing room – and it wasn't exactly Brisbane weather outside – and here

I was sweating up a storm, not through exertion but through uncontrollable nerves.

Five minutes before play is due to start at Lord's, a bell situated just below the visiting team's balcony rings out. The legendary Australian paceman Merv Hughes was over in his corner. A man known as much for his broad girth and droopy moustache as for his lion-hearted bowling, Merv was eyeing off the sandwiches on the table in the middle of the room when the bell pealed this first morning of the test.

'I think it's time for you two to go,' he said to me and Mark Taylor, before tucking into a second breakfast.

So away we went on that walk … You have to understand that it's an amazing journey just to get to the centre of the ground at Lord's, because there's no direct route. You go from the visiting team's dressing room down two flights of stairs into the famous Long Room, which is always packed with men wearing official-looking jackets and the celebrated egg-and-bacon tie of the Marylebone Cricket Club (or MCC). Then you have to make your way through the crowd from there. It's so old-fashioned – and so brilliant. I just tucked in behind Tubby, a veteran of this wayward Lord's journey, and followed him through the massing bodies.

'Good luck, chaps. You'll need it,' someone shouted to us. This was followed by 'See you in five minutes, old boy.' It was my first sledge in Test cricket – and it had come from the mouth of a member of the venerable MCC! Nothing could have made me more nervous than I was already, but these comments definitely increased my focus and determination. I was ready.

The first half-hour of my innings was a blur. Unlike most cricket grounds, where there's a roar as the bowler comes in for that first ball of a Test match, Lord's is enveloped in an eerie, deafening silence. Tubby played out the first over from England's fast bowler Andrew Caddick and I got ready to face the next, from Neil Foster. Caddick was a rising star, quickly gaining respect from opposition batsmen, while Foster, who was best known for his ability to swing the ball, was in his twilight days.

The first ball from Foster was full on my leg stump, and I leaned on it and clipped it through square leg. It ran down the famous Lord's slope which dips from the north side of the ground to the south, and rolled into the fence for four. It was the perfect start. And the day continued that way, despite one shaky moment when I was on about 20: I came down late on a ball from Caddick and rather than hitting it with the middle of the bat, I jagged it off the inside edge and French-cut it over the top of the stumps for another four. That was the only streaky shot I can remember.

The rest of my innings was, incredibly, just like my half-awake dream from the night before. I was on 50 when we came in at lunch, and well into the second session I remember looking up at the scoreboard and seeing that I was on 85. *I can get a hundred here, a century at Lord's*, I said to myself. It felt like a waking dream: my debut Test century in my second Test, at the home of cricket, no less.

From then on I had to work hard not to get ahead of myself and be distracted by the atmosphere and the signif-icance of what I now knew was possible. Yet I moved through the 90s fairly quickly, thank God, but it was a battle to maintain concentration. On 99 I turned one from Foster down to fine leg, took off down the pitch for the run to get my hundred, and, frankly, went berserk. It was an amazing feeling. It was the total fulfilment of all my dreams and sacrifices over two decades. At 23 years old I'd already had some great knocks; a variety of injuries; the bombshell dropped by my mother when she left me, Dad and my brothers and sister when I was twelve; and my struggles to adapt to the fast-paced life of Sydney after my upbringing in Wagga Wagga, in country New South Wales.

I took my helmet off and in an instinctive gesture planted a kiss on the Aussie coat-of-arms. This became my trademark on making a century. On that day at Lord's it was simply the best and most natural way I could express how I felt at such a proud moment of my cricketing career.

Although I made 152 over two days, and was on top of the world, I was still extremely disappointed to get out. All the same, the walk off the ground was memorable. It was every bit as remarkable as my first walk onto the pitch at Lord's the day before, but for totally different reasons. I knew it was a special moment and tried to savour every second. I received a standing ovation from everyone – the many Aussies there, and all the English punters as well. They seemed to have thoroughly enjoyed the innings and my stand of 260 with Tubby.

As I approached the pavilion I saw that all the MCC members – the same ones I'd walked through the day before to start my innings, even the sledgers – were on their feet, applauding. I was rapt. And I will never forget going into the Long Room: there was a tremendous applause that felt very intimate and personal because the room was packed and there were members all around me.

'Well played, lad,' I heard a few of these gents say, which felt a lot different from yesterday's 'Good luck … You'll need it.' Then I skipped up the two flights of stairs to the dressing room, feeling as though I was walking on air. My team-mates were all waiting for me near the door and within minutes everyone had come over to shake my hand. They had even written my name and score on a strip of tape and stuck it on the Honours Board in the Lord's Pavilion; later on they would be engraved there forever.

Even as I look back today, many years and many runs down the line, I'm not sure which Lord's walk is the most vivid and unforgettable for me: threading my way through that crazy maze to get onto the ground to start batting, past the MCC members, while trying to keep up with Tubby; or the proud walk back to the sheds, knowing that I'd scored my first Test hundred and had truly done my bit for the team.

All I can say for sure is that innings was one of the most unforgettable experiences I've ever had while wearing the baggy green cap for Australia. After all I'd been through in my short life till then – the peaks and troughs of batting, my family's coming apart, the pain of living away from my fiancée, my injury traumas – I now truly felt that I belonged.

Chapter 1

Living on a Prayer

1970–1985

I'm one of a family of six. My siblings are Julian, who is 41 at the time of writing, Tracey, 40, and Mark, who is 30. I'm 35. My mother Carole was pregnant with Julian when she and Dad got married. In her teens at the time, Mum had qualified as a nurse in her native Wales and then moved for work to Newcastle-upon-Tyne, on the north-eastern coast of England. Soon after Julian's birth my parents had Tracey, who was also born in England, but in 1966 the four Slaters migrated by boat to Australia.

They'd been tempted to go to Canada because Dad had been offered a job there, but when a second offer came through for a job in Launceston, Tasmania, they quickly decided on that instead. The Australian offer was a better option because Dad would start to receive his salary on embarkation and a house was included in the package. So off they sailed for Tasmania. Dad taught high school

9

agriculture/science at his new posting in Launceston, the same subject he'd taught since graduating from college. After three years in Launceston they shifted to Wagga Wagga, in rural New South Wales, where Dad became a lecturer in agriculture at what is now Charles Sturt University. For a while we lived in the housing provided by the university for the lecturers, known as 'Nappy Alley' because so many newborn babies lived there. I added to the reputation of Nappy Alley when I was born, Michael Jonathon Slater, on 21 February 1970.

Wagga Wagga was a great place to grow up, for many reasons. It was a good size – it had a population of around 50,000 when we moved there – and it was in the country, with a great Australian climate, so it was a real outdoor kind of place. But the best thing about it as far as I was concerned was the amazing amount of sport played there and the exceptional number of sportsmen and women who'd grown up in the surrounding Riverina area – some of whom I'd one day call team-mates, such as Mark Taylor and Geoff Lawson, the great Test fast bowler, NSW captain and one of my future mentors.

My family was always involved in sport, so from an early age it just seemed natural for me to play any game that was on offer. As a young boy, my philosophy was this: anything for a game. I didn't know, of course, that the game of cricket would become my life – how could I when I was so young and green?

Growing up, I spent lots of time in and around sporting grounds. Mind you, this was nothing unusual for a kid growing up in a large Australian country town. Julian and

Tracey were keen swimmers, and even in primary school they'd be up at 5.30 am most mornings, training at the pool that was just down the street from where we lived. One of my friends, Andrew Sharrock, was a very good swimmer and I would go to swimming lessons with him. Although I was pretty good in the pool, swimming was not something I especially enjoyed and the lessons never grabbed me. It was all too solitary for me. I found I naturally gravitated to team sports.

Strangely enough, I wasn't the kind of kid to have posters of my sporting heroes plastered all over my bedroom walls. But I did have my cricketing idols. Aussie Test players such as Dennis Lillee and Rod Marsh were giants to me, as were Greg Chappell, Allan Border and Kim Hughes, whose batting I hugely admired. And I loved to watch the two West Indian openers, Gordon Greenidge and Desmond Haynes, tear up attacks. I'd spend hours picking apart their techniques and getting my head around exactly how they batted. These were the kinds of guys that made me hope to play cricket some day at the highest level.

But my biggest hero was Vivian Richards, the West Indian Master Blaster. I loved his cocky attitude as much as his batting. I even pretended to chew gum, just like him, so that when I batted I could feel just that little bit closer to the guy. Viv was incredible. Years later, I finally got to meet him when I toured with Australia to the West Indies in 1995. We met in Antigua, his hometown, which even has a street named after him. I'd never been more nervous in my life. But Viv just shook my hand and said in his deep, super-cool West Indian accent, 'Michael, I love the

11

way you play, man.' Talk about a natural high. I was totally awestruck.

Being English, my father played soccer, and I followed his example, turning out for the Wagga United Crows. I mostly played as a centre forward … I've always liked to be on the attacking side of a team. I soon picked up hockey as well, which was my best sport apart from cricket. Dad, Mum, Julian and Tracey all played hockey, and later my younger brother Mark took up the game. Hockey was like most of my sporting interests, including golf − if my parents or my siblings were into it, I followed suit.

In the summer, though, it was cricket for me from very early on in my life. Dad had been a good cricketer in England, playing for Rawtenstall in the renowned Lancashire League. He had just started to make a name for himself as a talented bowling all-rounder when, at the age of nineteen, he decided to give up his possible cricketing career to attend university. He only played occasionally after this, but when he arrived in Wagga Wagga he played at club level − and when I grew older, for a few seasons we actually faced up to each other in opposing Wagga teams, which made for some strange encounters.

As a kid, I was ultra-competitive. I had to win. I had to be the best at whatever I did, especially if it involved sport. Coming second just wasn't acceptable to me and this was an attitude that stayed with me for years. Of course the flipside is that there were times when my competitiveness in sport wasn't very healthy. There were occasions when I'd be furious with myself for getting a low score in cricket, or shout at a hockey team-mate who'd made a mistake. At times I must have been a difficult person to play alongside.

During primary school we'd play cricket on Saturday mornings and my father was always involved, often umpiring at square leg. One day when he was umpiring I was run out without facing a ball – the most bitter pill for any batsman to swallow – and it was Dad who gave me out from square leg. Of course, I totally spat the dummy. I threw my bat away as I walked off the ground, moaning that I wasn't out. I then spent the rest of the innings sulking in my father's car.

When we got home that evening, Dad got stuck into me – which just wasn't in his nature at all. Mum was always more the disciplinarian; Dad had a softer nature, he was more likely to try to talk things through rather than get mad at me. But on this memorable day he told me that if I ever behaved like that again I wouldn't be allowed to play *any* sport. I was completely stunned. He'd never been that tough with me before.

This was a genuinely significant event in my young life. My father taught me a lesson I've always remembered. While my competitiveness and passion to succeed have stayed close to the surface, I did begin to realise I had to try to control my emotions thanks, in part, to Dad's lecture. But my will to succeed was also the reason I was able to harness whatever early talent I had and stay motivated to work hard at any sport I played. It was a fine balance, the one between the positive and negative aspects of my passion to succeed – a balance I was constantly working at to achieve – and there were certainly times throughout my sporting life when that passion spilled over and made for some genuinely unpleasant moments.

I'm not sure where this competitiveness came from, but even when playing backyard cricket with Dad, Julian and Mark, which we did a lot, they soon noticed my competitive streak. In those days we'd moved off the university campus, away from Nappy Alley, to 17 Hardy Avenue, Wagga Wagga, a small house with a decent backyard, perfect for our very own Test matches. We had some amazing cricket battles out in that back garden. We'd place different markers around the yard, each marker denoting a different number of runs, and you'd have to hit the marker to score a certain amount of runs. Over the fence, of course, was six and out. Without knowing it at the time, I guess this early practice aiming for those backyard markers helped me with my placement later on.

But often our games got a little too competitive and would end in an argument, usually between me and my elder brother Julian. When I got out I just couldn't accept it, and Julian would storm inside, shouting behind him that he'd never play with me again, until I learned how to be a good sport. I couldn't handle getting out – I loved batting and hated failing so much that I could never believe I was out. Even if my stumps were spread-eagled all over the ground, I *still* didn't believe I was out!

So my elder brother would give up on me, abandoning our backyard test match, and I'd end up in tears. But Julian was as keen a cricketer as I was, so it generally wasn't long before he'd give in and return outside to resume our battles. Ultimately though, he wasn't as driven as I was and he was more willing and able to adhere to the rules – whereas for me, what mattered most was winning. I had to be the best.

● ❶ ●

When I started playing sport, there were lots of good coaches who were well qualified and knew their sport, and parents who were very willing to give their time and support to their children. I was certainly incredibly lucky to have a father who became very involved with all my teams. He was a completely committed and loving father … even if he did give me out the day I had that tantrum!

When I was young it seemed to me that every sport ever invented was played in Wagga, so kids like me could always find one they liked. Geography had something to do with this range of sports, too. Being halfway between the big eastern capitals of Sydney and Melbourne, Wagga embraced the favourite sports of both state capitals: strong rugby league, rugby union and Aussie rules, and lively cultures in all three. This was unusual, because most NSW towns were either league or union – and in Victoria it was Aussie rules or nothing. The rugby league Mortimers came from Wagga, so did Aussie rules stars Paul Kelly and Wayne Carey. As for cricket, Geoff Lawson came from Wagga, and Mark Taylor played all his junior cricket there, so naturally we claimed him too, even though he was born in Leeton, about 130 kilometres to the north-west. These legendary sportsmen were great role models for younger guys like me. We could see that if we were good enough and worked hard enough we could go all the way to the top – and I could see a clear pathway from rural Wagga to national and international success.

Without a doubt, one of the strongest influences on my cricket was local coach Warren Smith. From the time I was seven, Warren was my personal coach and advisor. He is one of those no-nonsense country blokes, with a strong, direct gaze, who has only to look you in the eye to convey his commitment and passion. And what's more, he's a redhead, with all the fieriness that goes with red hair.

My big brother Julian went to Monday afternoon cricket sessions run by Warren, so, naturally enough, I soon followed him. I received my first formal cricket coaching at the age of seven and Warren remained my personal coach until I was about eighteen, when I left Wagga to go to the Australian Cricket Academy (now known as the Commonwealth Bank Cricket Academy). Warren and I are still close today – and there have been times in my life when he's been almost like a surrogate parent to me.

Warren Smith was a technically minded coach and his style appealed to the perfectionist in me – perfectionism and competitiveness are two attitudes that seem to me to be joined at the hip. Even at that early age, I sensed Warren wasn't just teaching me the basics, he was good enough to refine my batting. He spotted my ability early on and often tells the story of how he saw me bat at one of my first Monday practice sessions. Warren was watching me hit balls being thrown to me by a few kids in the nets when he saw me hit what he thought was a perfect on-drive. He was curious, so he pulled me aside and threw a few more balls at me to see whether I could reproduce the shot. I did. From that moment on, as he's since said to many people, he knew that he had someone different on his hands.

He was an amazing coach, not just for me but also for Wagga and the whole Riverina area. Warren was always fair in how much time he devoted to each child, although I suspect that he gave me a little extra time because he believed (or perhaps even knew) that there was something special about the way I played. Warren had such a passion for cricket − I was very lucky so early in my life to have come across someone who understood the game so well and who was so committed to it.

Warren valued quality fielding, too, and made fielding practice a priority in his sessions. He would always remind me that you spend at least half the game in the field, so you should enjoy it − and the better you are at fielding, the more you'll enjoy it. His devotion back then to every aspect of the game was amazing, and that hasn't changed over the years, despite two heart attacks. Warren ended up coaching and working for NSW Cricket in various capacities, and later my Sydney club, the University of New South Wales, signed him up as club coach for the 2004/05 season. He was instrumental in helping them to win the one-day competition and reach the grade final that season (where they narrowly lost to the star-studded University of Sydney team). To have been able to guide my old First Grade team through to the finals in both competitions is a testament to Warren's extraordinary coaching ability, given that in my time the University of NSW only ever finished mid table at best. You can see why I call him 'the Super Coach'!

When I was eleven and in sixth class at Turvey Park primary school, I made the NSW Primary School Sports Association (PSSA) cricket and hockey teams, having represented the Riverina in the State Schools Champi-onships at both sports. It was a very big thing for me, as it would have been for any sports-minded youngster. My selection was totally unexpected. Apart from Warren's guidance and advice with cricket, it was the first time I'd had the feeling that someone had been watching me and had spotted some talent in me. Without fully realising where I wanted to go, my journey towards Test cricket – or hockey – had begun. Turvey Park was significant for me in another way: it was through some friends there that I met my childhood sweetheart, Stephanie Blackett, whom I later married.

The first time I made a NSW representative (rep.) team, outside of school teams, was in the Under-12 Division hockey in 1981. I then went on to make the Under-13, -15 and -17 NSW hockey teams. I was a left inner, which meant I was an attacking player who also helped out defen-sively, a combination of skills required by an opening batsman in cricket. Playing left inner also requires supreme fitness and I really enjoyed this aspect of the position. Hockey is a fast and skilful game and I fell in love with it instantly.

But while my sporting life, especially cricket, was progressing really well, there was trouble brewing at home. The biggest disruption to my young life came when my mother left us when I was twelve years old, at the start of 1983. It was totally unexpected and came completely out of the blue.

Now, when I think back, I realise there had been a lot of conflict in our household during the months leading up to the split, something that had never been the case before. I remember being woken several times by Mum and Dad yelling at each other. Often I'd hear someone crying and the other person storming off to bed. This was incredibly upsetting to me, but I still didn't believe that my parents would ever split up. As a kid you just don't imagine that sort of thing could happen to your family.

I can vividly recall the day Mum left. I came home from school one afternoon with my younger brother, Mark, and we found Dad in the front yard, crying. He was absolutely distraught. This shocked us. We'd never seen him cry before. I asked him what was wrong, and he replied, 'Your mother has left us.'

It hit us all very hard. Seeing my father so heartbroken hurt as much as knowing that my mother had gone. Being only twelve and Mark just seven, we were totally bewildered by this sudden, massive change in our life. Without warning, my special person – my mum – was gone. And we'd been close. I relied on her love, the affection that you can only get from your mother. Suddenly that was gone. There's no doubt that my mother's leaving has had a massive impact on me.

And it tore my father apart, to the point where he

needed sleeping tablets to get through each night. I'd never seen Dad so shattered – he looked like death warmed up. Not knowing where Mum had gone or whether she was coming back almost killed him. And she was nowhere to be found. As it turned out, Mum was still in Wagga, but we didn't discover that until a week or so later, when she eventually contacted us.

During the first few months of their split, my mother promised to come back. She said that she just needed some time for herself. But, sadly, it never happened. I didn't know it at the time, but she had formed a relationship with a work colleague named Barry Smith. I was fifteen or sixteen when I found out the real, full story and it filled me with resentment. It took me until my early twenties to get on top of that and to realise that I still loved her. But that was a long way in the future.

In fact, even though I later went through a tough divorce of my own, I still don't really understand why Mum did it. She has never sat down with us and talked it through. All I know is that it had a huge impact on my own life, and that of all my family. Things were never really the same following that fateful day she left.

People around us were as confused as I was. They'd always seen Mum and Dad – Carole and Peter Slater – as a great couple and loving parents. And as I've grown older it hasn't become any easier to understand how a mother of four could leave her family. Clearly, she must have been incredibly confused, and leaving must have seemed the right thing for her to do at the time. My own experience with divorce allows me to relate to this.

One hopeful day Mum called and said she would try to work things out with Dad. At the time, Tracey, her boyfriend Stephen, Mark, Dad and I were going on holiday to Surfers Paradise, and Mum promised that when we returned, she'd be back at home in Wagga waiting for us. I remember Dad seemed distracted during our holiday; he had no idea what to expect. But we kids were incredibly excited. After driving back from Surfers, I remember Mark and I running down the driveway, calling out for Mum. But when we reached the back door, it was locked. She hadn't come home at all. She did eventually arrive back home the next day, but she only stayed about a week. She didn't even unpack her bag.

A few days after she'd returned she suggested that Dad take us kids out for a game of golf. When we got home, she'd gone – this time for good. She'd moved with Barry Smith to Kempsey, about 400 kilometres north of Sydney; and later they moved to nearby Crescent Head, where we kids would sometimes go for holidays.

By then my older sister Tracey was in her senior year at high school, and she took on the motherly role, helping with the cooking and cleaning. It was a huge commitment, one that put a lot of pressure on her. I'll always be grateful to Tracey for having looked after us so well. And Dad is my hero. His courage and fighting qualities got him through the toughest period of his life. He set a fine example to us and never once lost his focus on raising his kids and guiding us through life.

Mum now lives in Newcastle, just north of Sydney, and she's married to Barry. I see her as often as I can and

I love her very much. I have a great relationship with Barry and with my father's second wife, Claire, whom he married in 1986, a few years after Mum left. It makes me happy knowing that both my parents are happy and are supported by loving partners and companions.

● ❶ ●

With Mum gone, my education began to suffer. I'd previously been just as driven with my education as I was with my sport. Up until about Year 9 I'd been an A-grade student, but I really began to slip after that, and soon sport was the only thing I could focus on properly. It became the best escape from all the drama we were going through. School became tricky in part because doing well at your studies and at sport was seen as really uncool. My large group of friends had begun to splinter into two opposing camps: one made up of the more serious, academic, sporting types, and in the other, those who tended to create or get into trouble.

Things began to go haywire and it started to get nasty. The tough crowd turned against me – I was receiving some recognition at school assemblies for getting into various representative sports teams and a few kids were giving me a hard time because of it. Two guys even formed an anti–Michael Slater group. So school became a bit stressful and I reacted by being disruptive in class, possibly trying to gain acceptance from the tough guys. I was beginning to hate school, and this combined with the anguish I was feeling about Mum leaving, and not knowing why, made me feel really insecure.

At school I was sometimes at the receiving end of physical attacks, not just verbal insults. There was a regular lunchtime game called 'pile-ons', in which as many kids as possible would pile onto someone they didn't like. One day I was targeted. A whole lot of kids piled on top of me and I couldn't breathe – I thought I was going to pass out. It shook me up badly so I decided to confront the ringleader, with whom I'd played cricket and hockey. I wondered if he had it in for me because he resented my sporting success. Just as I was about to have my first punch-up in the schoolyard I was, literally, saved by the bell – thankfully. I was no fighter.

When we went into the afternoon's woodwork class, there were whispers going around that some kids were planning to get me after school. I was petrified. During woodwork someone threw a metal rod with a pointed end at me. God knows what would have happened if it had hit me. It freaked me out and I made up an excuse to get out of the room. I bolted for home and spent the next few days at home nursing my bruised ribs. But I think the bruises on my psyche took longer to heal.

Chapter 2

It's My Life

1985–1989

In my early teens I began to see life as a struggle. After my parents split, nothing seemed certain anymore, and after the bullying at school, it seemed that life was just one big battle to survive. Never again could I take anything important for granted. The one thing I knew and had some confidence in was my ability at sport, especially cricket. Sport became my outlet and my sanctuary.

With my mother gone, Warren Smith and I became even closer. In some ways I gained a second father. My dad greatly appreciated the fact that Warren had taken a shine to me, and there was no doubt that Warren helped relieve some of the pressure on Dad during the tough period after Mum left. Warren would pick me up for training and drop me home afterwards in his old, beaten-up blue ute. During these drives he talked about a lot of things. Sometimes we'd even talk about what had happened with Mum – and although we didn't get too deep and meaningful, I think these talks helped me a lot. At the time I could easily have lost direction and fallen in with the bad crowd. Warren was a great mentor and positive influence on me, on and off the field. He always made a point of reminding me why I played sport in the first place: I loved it. And from the outset, he taught me that to succeed in anything you need to have a passion for it.

My younger brother Mark also suffered a lot after Mum's departure. He struggled to keep it together throughout his school years and became involved with the wrong sort of company more than once. It was such a shame. Mark was an amazing athlete, with just as much sporting talent and ability as I had, but because he was so much younger than I was when Mum left, sport hadn't become such a crucial part of his life in the way it had mine.

Throughout my school years my cricket progressed in tandem with my hockey, and I made various state teams in both sports. For a time I could fit both games into my year – cricket in the summer, hockey in winter. But soon enough, the cricket and hockey seasons started to overlap. My commitments in representative hockey came at the end of the winter season and they began to overlap with the beginning of the cricket season. I knew that at some stage I would have to choose one sport over the other, but I hoped to delay the decision for as long as I could.

However, someone else intervened to make my decision a little easier. Clive Robertson, a local schoolteacher, had a link with the AW Green Shield side for Balmain, a celebrated cricket club in inner-western Sydney. The Green Shield was an Under-16 competition, played over the Christmas holidays, in which each team was organised and selected by a First Grade club. The matches themselves were played on some of Sydney's best grounds and the standard of competition was high. It was one of the first steps towards men's First Grade cricket and beyond.

So when I was sixteen, I travelled to Sydney to play for Balmain in the Green Shield, along with a couple of other Wagga cricketers. I'd been to Sydney many times before. I'd played in sports carnivals and had enjoyed family holidays there, visiting Manly and other tourist places. But I still had that typical country boy attitude towards the city: it was the big smoke. It was too fast, the traffic was too crazy, and there was too much pollution. I just wasn't comfortable there. Sydney was fun, but it was just too different from Wagga for me. Yet I knew that if I wanted to progress with my cricket, one day I would have to think about moving to the city.

I was picked by Balmain to bat in the middle order, at number six. I didn't get a hit in the first game, but during the second game one of the opening batsman decided he didn't want to open and I was asked if I wanted his spot. Desperate for a bat, I said yes. Fortunately, I made some runs – and I'd open the batting for the rest of my career. The Green Shield was great. It exposed me to metropolitan cricket, which was a big thing for a kid from the bush, and I ended up being the leading run scorer in the competition that season. The following season the age group was changed to Under-17, so I played another season for

Balmain. Once again I topped the batting averages. Despite my reservations about Sydney, the Green Shield was a successful first stint for me in big-time cricket.

What I didn't realise as I played was that there were talent scouts and selectors watching those matches, and after my first season of Green Shield I was chosen for the NSW Under-16 side. What's more, I was made captain. That was a huge thing for me: I had been recognised as one of the state's best young cricketers. As a result I received a lot of publicity back home in Wagga. I'd captained a lot of teams before being made captain of the NSW Under-16s, from local sides to Riverina representative teams, so I'd had a considerable amount of experience – but being made captain of a NSW team was a huge honour. I couldn't believe it.

There I was, still sixteen at the start of the season, and after nearly ten years of playing cricket with genuine passion and commitment, I was captain of the NSW team, travelling across the country to the Australian championships. Because it was such a big moment and a great opportunity to impress people, I put a lot of pressure on myself in the lead-up to the matches. I badly wanted to do well with the bat and to lead the side in the manner expected of me. Unfortunately, the carnival did not go as well as I would've liked.

In the first couple of games I didn't make many runs. Instead of trying to work out what I was doing wrong, I became very negative about my batting and began to worry about not living up to expectations, and so in turn my captaincy suffered. I was just too intense about everything. Eventually I asked to bat down the order for the last couple of games. I'd allowed self-doubt to creep in and hamper my performance.

We ended up doing well in the carnival, but I returned home to Wagga quite disappointed with myself. I realised that I'd let the pressure get to me: I'd let my own expectations dominate my thinking and consequently had not played anywhere close to my ability. It was a tough but valuable lesson. Thankfully, Dad and Claire had travelled to the carnival all the way from Wagga by bus, a six-day round trip. It was wonderful to have Dad's support and encouragement through this tough time.

As I would learn, self-doubt is something that most cricketers battle with at various times in their career. Some of the best players in the world fight self-doubt every time they walk onto the field. It might not look like it – especially when you see someone like Viv Richards chewing gum and twisting the bat in his hands like an axe – but it's true. After all, a batsman is only ever one ball away from a mistake and failure, so every innings is a new challenge.

● ❷ ●

The following year, when I was seventeen, I had a freak, self-inflicted accident at school – I hit myself on my Achilles tendon with a rock. We'd been fooling around in class, throwing things up into the air and catching them behind our backs. Of course I had to push the game just a little bit too far. I found a huge rock, about the size of a bowling ball, which I threw into the air. But instead of catching it with my hands, I caught it on the edge of my Achilles tendon. I played a couple of hockey games soon after and limped off the field. It was then that I knew I'd done some serious damage. I had to have exploratory surgery before the Under-17 National Cricket Carnival, for which I'd been made vice-captain. Luckily I'd been in good form leading up to the carnival, so the NSW team coaching and management staff were very supportive.

I was sent to the Narrabeen Fitness Centre on Sydney's northern beaches before the carnival, where I had extensive physiotherapy every day. But unfortunately I couldn't get myself fit in time and was forced to withdraw from the carnival. It was another setback. There was an upside, however: it was at the Narrabeen Fitness Centre that I met Geoff Lawson, and he would later play a key role in my career.

I went to see an orthopedic surgeon about my tendon, Dr Peter Dewy, who gave me the biggest shock I'd had since Mum's departure. Dr Dewy examined my Achilles, looked me straight in the eye and told me that my dream of playing cricket for Australia was over. It was the worst thing I could have heard. It spelt complete disaster. I was down for days. But eventually I decided that I could get on top of it – although around this time Dad began to make a point of encouraging me to pay attention to my studies. I guess he was wondering if I could overcome my injury and was hinting that I might need to have a back-up plan, some kind of fall-back position if cricket didn't pan out as I'd dreamed.

But fortunately an operation eventually repaired my

Achilles tendon problem and the next year I was picked in the Under-19 state cricket side for the National Championships in Brisbane. I was a year younger than most of the team, which meant I was eligible to play again the following year. This was a double I'd always wanted to achieve. Playing for the state side that first year was a great opportunity because it allowed me to work with guys a year older, players I admired and respected. And when the captain of the side suffered an injury, I replaced him. This was another tremendous opportunity and a real vote of confidence in my cricket, given it was my first year in that talented company.

By this time, I'd had considerable experience as a captain. I'd led the Under-16 NSW team, and I'd been made the vice-captain of the NSW side the following year (although I didn't play, due to injury). Getting selected for the prestigious Under-19 competition was a cricketing milestone that over the years had led many players to first-class and Test cricket. But unfortunately, when I had my first turn in the Under-19 side I arrived at the carnival only to perform poorly once again, as did the whole team. I let the pressure get to me and underachieved with the bat. And I suspect that being a country boy from Wagga prevented me from gaining the respect as captain of the city boys in the side.

There was also an unpleasant incident over a letter I'd received from my girlfriend Stephanie Blackett while I was at the National Championships in Brisbane. While I was out, Steph's letter was intercepted by a couple of the players and they opened it and read the contents. Given her letter mentioned a few of the players in the side, this caused some real problems within the team.

Stephanie and I had first met in Year 7 on an Orientation Week camp at Berambula, just outside Wagga. Steph had been to a different primary school from me, Wagga Wagga Primary, but she knew some of the girls from Turvey Park, who introduced us. Her parents, Louise and Dennis, were well known in Wagga because they were a very theatrical family – they lived just opposite the Civic Theatre in town – and Louise had her own radio show. In Year 8 Steph and I started to spend more time together and formed a good friendship from that early age. At first we were just close friends, even though I sort of guessed she had a thing for me. I remember our first kiss at a school party in Year 9. After that I didn't speak to her for a few days. It was weird. I'm not sure why, but the aftermath just felt strange. I suppose I was shy and nervous.

I had a couple of other girlfriends in Years 9 and 10, but then a production of *Grease* changed everything. Stephanie and I both had roles in the musical: Steph played fast chick Rizzo and I played Dudie, one of the guys who hang round with Danny, the main character played by John Travolta in the film. We were stars for a week. It was fantastic. I ended up taking part in three songs for the production – I was given an extra role because no one wanted to play the Teen Angel during the corny 'Beauty School Dropout' number, so I put up my hand. Backstage I'd take off my Dudie gear and slip into my cricket whites and a gold vest, and I'd be transformed into the Teen Angel. Then I'd fly over the stage clinging to a rope like

Tarzan, swinging backwards and forwards. At the end of the number I'd take a huge tumble onto the stage, sending up the whole thing. It brought down the house every time. Steph and I became really close during this time. But then she started going out with a guy from another school, so I said to her, 'What's going on here? You and I had better go out.' We started dating from the age of seventeen, midway through Year 11.

From then on I began to spend so much time at Stephanie's house – I stayed there most nights after school – that Dad would sometimes call me 'the boarder' because I was never home. The Blacketts (Steph, her parents and brother Paul) definitely filled a void in my life. Her parents were very warm towards me and provided that motherly love I was missing. Once I even ran away to their house, after a fight with Dad's new wife Claire – you know, the usual 'You're not my mother, you can't tell me what to do' kind of thing. The Blacketts took me in for a day or two until I'd sorted things out at home. That's the kind of welcoming warmth they gave me.

On that trip to Brisbane as captain of the Under-19 side, I had phoned to tell Stephanie that I'd been struggling with a couple of the players who I felt didn't respect me as captain. Stephanie had written back saying that I should forget these guys and get on with my game. This was sound advice and I appreciated her support, but it wasn't that easy. When you're in a team that exists only for a couple of weeks, and you're with quite a few players you haven't met before, it's very different from dealing with guys you play alongside every Saturday and practise with every week. It's even worse when you're the captain and you're expected to stamp some authority on the side. My team-mates had passed around Steph's letter, which became really embarrassing for me and made me feel very, very vulnerable. What upset me wasn't so much what they said to me, but what I felt they were saying among themselves about me.

Fortunately, after these setbacks I had a turnaround the following year. I returned to the Under-19 NSW side as vice-captain for the 1988 carnival in Canberra. The lead-up to those championships had an extra edge for me because I'd found an article in Wagga's *Daily Advertiser* about the new Australian Cricket Academy in Adelaide (now known as the Commonwealth Bank Cricket Academy). I pasted the article in the special little book in which I'd write down all my career goals. This was something I'd done since about 1982, and continued to do until just before I was first dropped from the Australian team fourteen years later (and then, in late 1996, I started to write down my goals once more, which I think helped my comeback). I can't remember where the idea for the book came from, but it really helped me to focus.

From the moment I read that article in the *Daily Advertiser*, getting into the Australian Cricket Academy became my major goal. I saw it as a huge opportunity and a prestigious step in my career. It would enable me to live, breathe and eat cricket for almost an entire year (which began on 1 May and continued for eleven months, ending in April). I knew that if I did well in the carnival in Canberra I could make the Australian Under-19 side, and when you made that team you were automatically added to the Academy intake.

I started the carnival well, with a century in the first match. This was to become a pattern in my career. Once I learned how to handle the pressure I put on myself, I'd usually manage to make runs in the early games, often in the first innings. To do that in a Test series meant I could relax a bit, calm my emotions, keep my anxiety and insecurity in check, and get on with playing well.

I kept my form going throughout this carnival and scored a hundred against Victoria in the final, which we won: NSW claimed the National Championship and I had been one of the better performing batsmen. I think a left-hander from Canberra made the most runs in that carnival, some guy called Michael Bevan. We were both chosen in the Australian Under-19 squad. Finally I had achieved something I'd been working towards for several years. Despite some setbacks, self-doubt and occasional lapses in form, I was making tangible inroads towards my burning desire and goal of becoming a professional cricketer and playing for my country.

But first up I had to finish high school. I was glad to get out of there, especially after all the bullying that went on in Years 9 and 10. Those years were hell for me. But in Year 12 I was made school captain of Wagga High, which was a great achievement as well as being a real vote of confidence by my peers.

Drinks Break
Cars and Guitars

I guess I'll always be known as the guy with the red Ferrari, but my relationship with cars goes way back to my Wagga days. I've always loved cars – or anything with a motor in it, to be more accurate. From the time I was about seven, I'd spend my weekends with some friends on their family farm in Wagga, zipping around on their mini bikes. We'd get totally into it. Often bike riding would be all we'd do the whole weekend; we'd dash around the farm, come up with our own bike trails, jump creek beds and generally do wild stuff.

And I was a real daredevil, a genuine nutcase. Even though we'd be getting around on smallish bikes – 125 cc trail bikes and step-throughs, the zippy motorcycles (typically 90 cc) that have been a long-time favourite with Australia Post – I'm still surprised I was never seriously injured. My nickname was 'Mad Mike on the Motorbike', given to me by the mother of my mate (and later, best man) Neville Joliffe. She wasn't wrong.

As soon as I got my L-plates – I was the second person in my year to get them – I bought my first proper bike, a Suzuki ER185. It was a great bike. I used to ride it to school and cut through the hills along the way. Around that time I got into that perennial question that plagues car lovers: which is the better car, Holden or Ford? Personally, I was pro-Holden. My Dad had a green Holden Kingswood, which he eventually traded in for a Commodore, so I had to support Holden. It made for some pretty exciting shouting matches when we'd all sit down to watch the annual Bathurst 1000, the Australian Touring Car Championship round that was heavily contested by Holdens and Fords.

I always knew that one day I'd have a nice car – a *really* nice car – but that was some way off in the future. The first car Steph and I bought together was a Ford Meteor, which I loved (although I now realise it was a terrible car), and we kept it for a couple of years. It was a great car – except when you hit a speed of around 110 kilometres an hour, at which point it would vibrate madly like an out-of-control washing machine. When I started playing first-class cricket I bought a Honda CRX two-door, a little hatchback that went like the clappers. Mind you, I understood the benefits of defensive driving and I wasn't a dangerous driver, I was just keen to put my foot down.

When I was selected for the Australian cricket team, one of the many perks that resulted was a deal I struck up with the Mazda Sports Club. In exchange for a few promotional appearances they'd give me a great car. I'd drive it for 8000, maybe 10,000 k's, and then I could change it over. I drove three or four different Mazdas during that time, starting with a Mazda 626, a pretty conservative set of wheels, and eventually moving on to an MX6, which was a pretty flash car.

I was so turned on by Mazdas that I bought a red Mazda RX7, one of only 25 cars that had been modified in Mazda's race-car garage so you could drive them on the road as well as the track. It was so much better than the regular RX7. It had a great shape, a twin-turbo rotary engine, and it went really quickly. This was the first 'serious' car that I owned, the kind of car a real buff would admit to driving. It was also a hard car to drive – it would 'tramline' if you hit a groove in the road, which made it tough to control. But I loved the experience of really *driving* – rather than just steering – a car. That's one of the main reasons I got into serious cars: I can't get enough of that sensation of being in complete harmony with the car and the road.

Losing that Mazda was one of the saddest days of my car-owning life. It happened while I was in England on the 1997 Ashes tour, where I didn't play much cricket. It was stolen. I'd returned it to Mazda for a respray and a service, but someone pinched it. Four months later it was found stripped for parts and burned out. I was devastated – I loved that car. Here I was on an incredibly disappointing cricket tour and someone had stolen my great car while I was away. It was a pretty bad time.

When you really get into cars, the first rush of driving an amazing set of wheels fades fairly quickly and you soon start pondering that fatal question: 'What next?' But with the RX7 I hadn't reached that stage – I definitely hadn't finished with that car. But luckily it was insured. With the payout I bought a BMW M Roadster, a real pocket rocket with a 3.2-litre engine (like the one Australian cricketer Michael Clarke now drives). It was the first convertible I'd ever owned. At the time I was managed by a group called Promotional Partners. Peter Adderton ran the company and his brother Matthew looked after my day-to-day concerns. We became great mates, and still are today. Peter was the one with the money – he was also a serious car nut and would let me drive some great cars. One day he lent me a Ferrari 355, adding: 'Don't worry, it's insured. Just go out and have a good time.' How could I resist? I was now able to live out every car-obsessed boy's dream of jumping into a Ferrari, and it was one of the biggest kicks of my life. The Ferrari was a real driver's car. I said to Peter, 'I'll have one of these in the next five years.'

Peter has a lot to answer for, because through him my love for cars was fanned into a burning desire, a real obsession. And it's a very expensive habit. I opened a Ferrari account and started putting away money specifically for the purchase of my dream car.

There's a showroom on William Street, in inner Sydney's Kings Cross, which is the place to find Ferraris. There I began my negotiations for a Ferrari – a Le Mans Blue 355, the best of the 355s they had – which I intended to lease. But one night I went out to dinner with Peter and he mentioned that he'd spotted two 355 Ferrari Spiders in the window of Bevan Clayton's Mosman dealership. I couldn't wait. Straight after dinner we went window-shopping and two days later I drove out of the Mosman showroom in a red 355 Spider.

It was a fantastic day. Bevan Clayton took me for a lap of the block, to make sure I understood the car, and then I was away. I know there's a lot of talk about Ferrari drivers and their small penises and big egos, you know the kind of thing … But as a genuine car lover who doesn't drive too badly (I've qualified for a racing licence), the sheer pleasure of driving that car was indescribable. I get the same feeling with the blue Ferrari that I now drive. I just love it.

People sometimes ask me what is the point of owning such a fast car, given that our speed limits are relatively low compared to Europe. My usual response it that it's really fun getting to the speed limit as quickly as possible – 'I can get to the limit quicker than you!' The 355 can go from 0 to 100 klicks an hour in 4.6 seconds. That is some serious speed. And also, for me the actual engine 'note', its hum, is music to my ears. It really sings. Most 355 drivers, myself included, don't need a stereo. We get off just by listening to the engine, it's such a beautiful noise.

And the other great thing is that I get my car onto a racetrack a few times a year. I take it out to Eastern Creek Raceway in western Sydney — and when you come roaring down that straight, doing 220 kilometres an hour, you really get to understand what that car can do, the magnificence of its power and engineering. It's also really good to get that urge for speed out of your system.

Strangely enough, when I first made the Australian cricket team, the other players were a really conservative bunch when it came to cars. They all drove Commodores and tame cars like that, although Warnie did own a Ferrari 355 before I got mine.

You could probably say that there's a connection between my need for speed and the aggressive way I batted: the desire to score runs quickly, at genuine pace, is a lot like the urge to drive a sports car. But as I matured as a player I realised that there were times on the cricket pitch when I needed to be cautious. In my cricket, occasionally I needed to drive a Commodore, so to speak.

●●●

Music is another one of my life-long passions. When I was growing up, I used to raid my older brother's record collection, which was packed with bands like Split Enz, Cold Chisel, ELO and Supertramp. Then my sister Tracey's boyfriend (now husband) Stephen turned me onto Dire Straits' *Making Movies*, which became my favourite album. One Christmas I was given a portable tape player and after that I spent all my spare time taping all the records I loved so much.

Stephen also played the guitar and he'd bring his acoustic around to our place. We'd all totally get into the music. I later taught myself to play the guitar, but I wish I'd learned to play it earlier in my life. I genuinely think that I'm a frustrated rock star trapped in a cricketer's body!

In March 1996, during the World Cup tour to India, I started learning to play the guitar – I had loads of spare time because I wasn't playing any one-day cricket. I was walking through Mumbai when I drifted into a music shop ... and before I knew what I was doing, I'd bought a dodgy guitar, a chord book and a songbook. I then spent every moment of that tour, when the team didn't need me, alone in my room studying the chord book.

The first song I mastered was The Troggs' 'Wild Thing' – but it was 'Wild Thing' with a twist. I'd make up my own different versions, changing the lyrics each time to comment on the differ-ent players in the team. From then on, during most games I'd put on my 'Wild Thing' performance, and it went down pretty well.

The NSW all-rounder Shane Lee was also on that tour of India, and he's a very accomplished guitarist. When we returned to Sydney after the tour I started hanging out with Shane, his brother, the bowler Brett Lee, and some other guys at a rehearsal space in Pyrmont – this was the first version of their band Six And Out. I would have loved to join their band, but it never tran-spired. I'm forever dirty with them. I still sometimes say to Shane: 'You needed me! You shouldn't have dumped me.'

The guys still play from time to time, and I sometimes get up and sing along with them. The trouble is, I always join in towards the end of the night after I've had a few drinks, and I can never remember the words to any of the songs. I'm forever trying to sing Green Day's 'Basket Case', but I always balls it up. On a few occasions they even turned my microphone down on stage, without telling me. When I'd complain between songs that my mic was too low, they'd assure me the crowd could hear me. And when I eventually found out what they were doing, Shane insisted I'd been playing the unplugged version. Bastards!

Without doubt my biggest musical heroes are Bon Jovi (hence my decision to use the titles of some of their songs for this book's chapter titles). I first heard them when I was in Year 10, and three years later I went to see them with Michael Bevan, when we were at the Australian Cricket Academy in Adelaide. They were playing at the Adelaide Tennis Centre, just around the corner from where Bevo and I were living, near the Adelaide Oval. Sure, the boys from Bon Jovi had monster mullets, but their music was awesome and their stage show was incredible. I've loved them from that moment on.

I've now seen Bon Jovi live nine times and I finally got the chance to meet my heroes after a show at Milton Keynes, north of London. Through Shane Warne I'd met Rod McSween, who helped organise Bon Jovi's UK shows, and he gave me tickets to a show with access to the on-stage VIP area. (I stood on that stage looking out over a sea of faces and felt the amazing thrill it must be to play in a rock band.)

At the end of the show, Rod McSween sent me a text message telling me to wait in the moshpit area. Rod turned up to get me after about twenty minutes. I thought I'd be one of scores of people schmoozing about backstage, but there were just two others apart from me. We had our own personal audience with the band. It was great. The first person I met was Heather Locklear, the American TV star married to the Bon Jovi guitarist Richie Sambora. I hung around with them for half an hour, sipping beers with the guys. I found it an incredible experience. It's always risky meeting your idols — what if they turn out to be complete wankers? — but meeting Bon Jovi was a genuine thrill. They were all lovely guys. After a while I realised I hadn't met the man himself, Jon Bon Jovi, who'd been off signing autographs.

It's hard to underestimate how big a fan I am of 'JBJ', as the following story demonstrates. I once saw a photo of Jon on the cover of a Bon Jovi book and noticed he had a Superman tattoo on his left shoulder. It happened to be at the time I was planning to get a tattoo. There are no prizes for guessing which tattoo I went with.

Any CD by Bon Jovi was of course the first CD I'd reach for in the dressing room after we'd won a game — that is, once we'd dispatched with John Williamson's mandatory Aussie classic 'True Blue' and Cold Chisel's rock anthem 'Khe Sanh'. I'd usually go for something like 'Always' or 'Living on a Prayer'. Then guys like Damien Fleming or Jason Gillespie would take over with the really heavy music. It didn't work for everyone though — Mark Waugh was always one of the first to start complaining about the noise levels and the intensity of the music. Before we could object, Mark would take over the boom box and play something safe — and quiet — like Daryl Braithwaite's 'Horses'. It wasn't Bon Jovi, that's for sure.

When I finally did get to meet Jon, he came over, we were introduced, and all I could think about was, *Should I show him the tattoo?* I really wanted to but it also seemed a bit wanky. Eventually I realised that I'd regret it for the rest of my life if I didn't show him the tatt, so I rolled up my sleeve and flashed him my ink-work. He looked at my arm, looked at me, rolled his eyes and said, 'Yeah, good on you.' I felt like a complete dill – but it was one of the best moments of my life.

Chapter 3

Stick to Your Guns

1989–1990

Before I joined the Australian Cricket Academy in Adelaide, which was then in its second year, I was part of the Australian Under-19 team that played a three-week series against New Zealand in Australia. Beginning in late February 1989, the series consisted of some one-dayers, followed by three 'Tests', in Mildura, Adelaide and Melbourne. The New Zealand team included all-rounders Chris Cairns and Chris Harris, and batsman Mark Richardson (then playing as a left-arm spinner). These three guys were impressive cricketers and future Test players.

I struggled for runs in the one-dayers — a portent of the problems I was to have later with my position in the one-day team, perhaps. But I made a big century in the Second Test in Adelaide, which was an important innings for me. I was 198 not out overnight. A double century was screaming out my name. Typically, I let my enthusiasm get the better of me and was run out first thing the next morning without further bothering the scorer. But at least I'd already made a big score, instead of one of my regular carnival failures. I was disappointed not to get 200, which would have been my first ever, but my 198 was still the highest individual score of that series. I backed it up in Melbourne with 70 in tricky, wet conditions, and finished up being the highest scorer in the Australian side. It was a wildly successful series for me and coach Jack Potter predicted that I had a bright future.

Because I made the Australian Under-19 team I was offered a spot in the Australian Cricket Academy in the 1989/90 intake. Some of the other guys in my year included Brendon Julian, Michael Bevan and two players – Craig White and Martin McCague – who ended up playing for England. (Many years later I think I might've played a role in messing up Martin's brief Test career, by taking to his bowling in his only Test match.) Future first-class players such as Stuart Law, Darren Berry and Jamie Cox had been part of the first year's group at the Academy, so it already had a big reputation.

But to attend the Academy, and in the process take my cricket further, I had to move to Adelaide for a year. The idea of leaving my family and home for the first time in my life for an extended stretch was daunting and pretty scary. But after talking it through with Dad and Stephanie, I decided that this was a challenge I needed to take.

Our daily schedule at the Academy began at 7.30 am, when we'd be picked up by a minibus and taken to the

North Adelaide aquatic centre, where we'd train before returning at 9 am. Then in the afternoon, from 4 to 6 pm, we'd practise in the nets or work on some cricket-specific skills. The activities during these time slots changed daily. This routine left the middle of the day free, so we could get away from the Academy and from each other for a while – and make a little money. We were all living in dormitory rooms at St Mark's College, directly opposite the most beautiful cricket ground in the world, Adelaide Oval. However, the Academy didn't line up jobs for us – we had to go out and find our own.

So I arrived in Adelaide a week before everybody else, in order to find some work. I'd heard that a couple of guys in the previous intake, including Jamie Cox, had worked in a bank, and that sounded all right to me. Otherwise I thought I'd get a job at the airport or as a courier racing around the city. But once I was in Adelaide, with no one else around, I felt so lost and lonely that I ended up making myself known to the people at the Australian Institute of Sport (AIS), which ran the Academy – and then caught a bus straight back to Wagga for a few days. When I returned to the Academy all the other guys were there and I settled in much more comfortably.

In its early days the Academy was a godsend for cricket in Australia and it was soon admired around the cricketing world. That was particularly the case in England, whose cricketers were desperate to drag themselves out of a lengthy slump. The English administration looked on as the Academy helped to revitalise Australian cricket after the grim days of the mid 1980s. In the first few years of its existence the Academy had the best young players in the country, players talented enough to move quickly into first-class cricket. Some had even played a few Sheffield Shield games before arriving in Adelaide. While I think the Academy has sometimes received too much credit for helping players' careers, it did give me the chance to concentrate intensely on cricket for a year, and helped me to mature faster as a player.

The Academy had set up an interesting system for its players' future selection at state level: if the South Australian selectors wanted to select an Academy player, they first had to ask the player's home-state selectors if they were thinking about selecting him. If the home state wasn't interested, then South Australia had first dibs. This is how Michael Bevan came to play his first Sheffield Shield game for South Australia, a match in which he scored a hundred.

South Australia had it made at Shield level for a few years – it created quite a stir with the other states when they realised that some of their most talented youngsters were staying in Adelaide after finishing at the Academy, having been poached by South Australia. We had such a great lifestyle in Adelaide, which is like a big country town, and this made it easier for players to stay put – particularly those who, like me, came from the bush. I think if South Australia had shown a genuine interest in me as a player, I would have seriously considered staying. I loved the feel of Adelaide, to me it was very similar to Wagga.

In its own way, the Academy was a great finishing school (although the format has changed since I was there).

In my time you were there for almost twelve months, training morning and afternoon, and trying to get your head around such concepts as sports psychology, which was new to us all. There was a lot of emphasis at the Academy on the mental side of the game; they also focused on fitness and enhancing particular skills. The program attempted to look at cricket in a more professional manner than had previously been the case and, as long as you dedicated yourself to it, you could cram three playing years' worth of sporting development into one.

At first, I'd been petrified about going to Adelaide. The realisation that I was leaving my comfort zone, my support base, was quite frightening. But I settled in well enough. Steph would come across at least once a month on the Greyhound bus from Wagga, which made Adelaide feel a little more like home. She'd found a solid job at Grace Bros and was still comfortable back in Wagga, but I loved her visits. As for me, I'd finally snared both a job and a bat sponsorship at the same time, which was quite a coup.

Duncan Fearnley, the UK bat manufacturer, had a warehouse in the Adelaide hills, and I scored a job there packing orders for about five hours every day, in between Academy training sessions. On the weekend, when I'd play cricket for Adelaide University, I'd use Duncan Fearnley bats. I even scored a hundred in a game against East Torrens, who were led by the legendary David Hookes – one of the most aggressive middle-order batsmen ever to play for Australia – which was the only time I'd ever get to play against him. So I was set: I had my room at the college, a bat sponsorship deal, and I was getting around in a Jaffa-orange Mazda Capella, a Slater family car I'd inherited. Despite the odd pangs of homesickness, I was tickled pink.

When I wasn't driving the Mazda, Michael Bevan and I would ride around the city on bicycles that we'd been given. It was great exercise, and Adelaide is a pretty easy city to get around, far easier than Sydney or Melbourne. But one Saturday morning, two weeks after I'd arrived in this new city, we rode up to the aquatic centre for a swim and a gym session (we were both into gym and general fitness work). As we rode back to the Academy, I was in front of Michael coming down O'Connell Street in North Adelaide. Suddenly a car cut across me and flew into a service station. My bike got caught up in its back bumper and I hit the ground very hard, with my left hip taking the impact. It all happened very quickly. I was in a lot of pain and really shaken up.

The two young guys in the car had a pile of beer on the back seat and seemed to be rushing to a party, but they ended up driving me back to our rooms at St Mark's. I had cuts and bruises and a severe pain in my hip, so I lay low for most of the day. The next day Brendon Julian took me to get some scans and x-rays but nothing was picked up. The official verdict was 'heavy bruising'. The officials at the Academy were notified and kept an eye on me.

This injury and its after-effects dogged me for the remainder of my stint at the Academy, which quickly went from being a time of real opportunity to a year of huge disappointment and hardship. After the collision, I was sent to Canberra for a couple of sessions of intensive physiotherapy at the Australian Institute of Sport. I also spent some time in Melbourne with physiotherapist Jeff Mackie. I'd stay at his place for a week at a time to receive treatment. In Adelaide I also saw doctors and orthopedic surgeons regularly, but nothing seemed to make much difference. At one stage I was even put into hospital so I could be manipulated under anaesthetic. The doctors thought this would release some nerves and ease the pressure in my sacroiliac and facet joints. For a few days there seemed to be some improvement, but it didn't last and soon enough my hip returned to its pre-treatment condition.

So I flip-flopped between periods when I was able to train and times when I just wasn't fit enough to do much at all. It was very frustrating; all this treatment didn't seem to be getting me anywhere. And the pain could be excruciating – it would often take me until lunchtime before I was loose enough to move without too much discomfort. I found the condition extremely debilitating.

Eventually I was diagnosed with ankylosing spondylitis (AS), a condition I've suffered from ever since. Normally, AS starts with acute swelling of the lumbar area and can be set off by a specific event – in my case, the bike accident was probably the trigger. Over time, if you're not active, your spine can stiffen up to the point where the vertebrae actually fuse together. A lot of old people you see hunched over have suffered from AS throughout their lives. I feel their pain, literally.

I struggled through the remainder of the Academy year. Being at the Academy was an ambition that I'd achieved only to have it thwarted by a stupid accident. I was ambitious and it was a substantial setback for me – but there were some positives that came out of the experience. The frustration forced me to develop a mental toughness that in turn helped me to cope with the pain, allowing me to participate in the Academy program when I often felt like going easy on my back. It was an ordeal that required a lot of inner strength, a quality that every Test cricketer needs.

I wasn't able to play some games and I also missed tours because I had to stay behind to receive treatment. It was like coming down with the mumps during the school holidays and not being able to play every day with your mates. As a batsman, I struggled with my footwork because of my AS condition. Eventually I went on the final tour of the Academy year, to New Zealand, and managed to get through it all right. I even scored heavily in a couple of matches.

But my main learning experience was very different from that of the other guys, who were able to concentrate purely on cricket. I had to learn to cope with a serious injury and deal with the frustration that caused as it slowly spread from my back into other parts of my body. At times I thought I was going to be told to go back to Wagga, and sometimes I felt like that was what I wanted to do; it was so difficult to sit there and watch the other players in the nets or out on the field. And there was also my long-distance relationship with Steph drawing me back to Wagga – sometimes I'd start to think that life back home would be much easier, much more comfortable.

Peter Spence, the assistant coach at the Academy, would get me to operate the bowling machine at practice but frankly, I found that boring. He also taught me how to use a computer program that documented a match ball by ball, and is now used all over the cricketing world. The trouble was that he would delegate that pretty tiresome job to me at most games, which as far as I was concerned just rubbed it in that I was injured and not fully part of the program.

But my final act as an Academy player provided a rare highlight. It was an innings in Perth that set me back on course and also proved crucial in the development of my batting. Looking back, this knock followed a pattern that so often occurred throughout my career: when things were going badly – such as when I was a kid putting too much pressure on myself at a representative carnival, or when I was struggling with my back problem – somehow I'd eventually manage to turn things around and move a few steps forward. I would struggle, mark time, then burst out of a slump and jump a few hurdles in double-quick time. It was nerve-wracking but at least I was continuing, gradually, to move towards my goal of playing for Australia.

Late in the Academy year, desperate to get out on the field, I made myself available and was chosen for the team to play in Perth, against a WA Second XI. I was still struggling physically – fielding was a nightmare – and was finding it hard to move freely at the crease. From an early age I'd been known for my quick and decisive footwork, so it was frustrating to be stuck on the crease and forced to go at the ball rather than move myself into the best position to play it. But in this Perth game I got a start and suddenly began really going for my shots. I'd been a reasonably conservative batsman until then, only playing my full range of shots when I was well set, which was the traditional way of thinking about building a score. But on this day, without realising what I was doing, I just started to hit the ball hard – and it worked. I made a hundred in very quick time. In the process I'd discovered that there was another way for me to bat: I could actually take the attack to the bowlers before they'd had a halfway decent look at me.

That day was bliss. I hit the ball over cover, smashed it through point – suddenly I had liberated my batting and brought out the flair that I'd one day be known for. This innings was a turning point and, in a strange fateful way, had been brought about by my injury. So my lousy time at the Academy had ended on a high note, and the limitations imposed by the injury that had spoilt the year actually helped to take my batting to a new level.

On the strength of that one innings in Perth I was picked for a NSW Second XI game in Canberra in December 1989. In order to make the NSW game, I had to leave Perth on the red-eye special, the dreaded midnight flight, and I knew I'd be stiff and sore afterwards. I had a pit-stop in Melbourne, where my next flight was delayed. So by the time I arrived in Canberra mid-morning, not only had the game already begun, but I was in no condition to play my first 'adult' game for my state, a game the selectors would be watching closely. At least at the Academy everyone knew about my accident and my back problems, but that wasn't the case in Canberra with the NSW

Seconds side. It was also my first paid game – I played for the grand sum of $280, $250 of which I spent on a sapphire ring for Steph.

God knows what everybody thought of me. I knew I'd have to bluff my way through as best I could, but arriving late didn't help my nerves. Thankfully, team manager Noel Bergin told me to rest for an hour and get myself organised before going out to field. It was a good idea – although Noel wasn't to know quite how good.

I was very self-conscious when I was running, because I had this sort of wobble due to the pain in my back. My hips would actually sway when I walked or ran, and I looked anything but an athlete. I went out after the first drinks break and struggled in the field. My back had just about seized up and was sending a crazy sciatic pain shooting down my legs, but I tried to pretend that nothing was wrong. When I couldn't chase a ball properly or bend down to field another, the captain, Randall Green, abused me. To him, I was a young upstart who thought that just because I went to the Academy, I didn't have to try.

As a boy I'd won fielding awards, so this was pretty tough to handle. I was proud of my work in the field and it hurt that I couldn't do a good job for my new team, and that my captain and team-mates thought I wasn't putting in. I didn't want to explain what was wrong; it would've seemed like some poor excuse. It was tearing me up inside and I could imagine the selectors turning against me because of this.

But when we batted, I had a similar experience to the one in Perth: I went out and just blazed away, making a quick 130. And I timed the ball really well, even though my movements were restricted. Suddenly another bad game had turned around for me. By the end of the match, Randall and the others had changed their tune – they were even asking me to play for their clubs if and when I moved to Sydney. I might have bluffed my way through that match to some extent, but I was able to leave it feeling reasonably positive about my career.

Those two innings, in Perth and Canberra, were pivotal events for me, because they had shown me another way to play. Up until then I'd been an accumulator, someone who nudged around singles and waited for the right ball to hit. As a kid I was renowned for having a great little technique, something Warren Smith had both admired and polished. But now I knew I could take bowlers apart, which was a massive revelation. With my so-so year at the Academy ending on a surprisingly high note, I went home to Wagga for six months in a more positive frame of mind. I got a job working the bar at the Wagga Leagues Club, which I loved, and then, after a lot of thinking and talking with my father and Steph, I decided it was time to head to Sydney and try my luck in the big city.

Chapter 4

I Believe

1991–1993

I was pretty green when it came to life in a metropolitan city such as Sydney. The only time I'd spent there had been for cricket matches, holidays and junior carnivals, particularly the two seasons of Green Shield with Balmain when I was sixteen and seventeen. All I knew was that it was a hell of a lot different from sleepy Adelaide, the city of churches – and a world away from my hometown of Wagga. A move to live in the city on my own was a much bigger decision than my shift to the Academy for a year.

Yet I also knew that to improve my cricket and be recognised as a serious contender, I had to play in Sydney. After all, every talented bush cricketer from Sir Donald Bradman down has moved to the big city to further their career – as have many country kids in fields other than sport. But after returning home from the Academy I'd snagged that job as a barman at the Wagga Leagues Club. I enjoyed it and was eventually offered the chance to become an assistant manager. The offer was tempting and complicated my decision regarding Sydney. At one point, I even considered enrolling at Charles Sturt University in country NSW as a mature-age student, which I'd often thought of as a back-up plan to cricket.

But then I was offered a job with the NSW Cricket Association (or NSWCA), as it was then called – it's now just NSW Cricket. Neil Maxwell, a guy I'd played cricket against and who'd become a friend, was working at the NSWCA and had been spreading the word that they needed another young administrative officer. Neil put my name forward and I decided to go to Sydney to find out more about the job. If it panned out, it would help me make up my mind about shifting to Sydney. Dad and Steph were really supportive about my Sydney plans, even though they both knew how much distance – physical and emotional – it would put between us.

I took the bus to Sydney for the interview. It was a long day. At the offices in the city, on York Street, Neil introduced me to the legendary Bob Radford (now deceased), who was the secretary of the NSWCA. He was a one-man institution who'd been working there for what seemed like forever. The guy was a fine administrator and an amazing writer – and he was also a raging alcoholic, who'd come in early, put in five good hours of work and then spend the rest of the day at lunch, before retiring to the Cricketer's Club round the corner in Barrack Street and eventually riding the bus home. To me Bob was the big smoke squeezed into one larger-than-life character.

I got the shock of my life when we met. Neil Maxwell introduced us, and Bob's first comment was: 'Ah, you're the little motherfucker, are you?' I sat there, stunned, and said, 'Yes sir, no sir' as he swore like a sailor and asked me loads of strange questions. After that we had lunch and I went home to Wagga. During the bus trip back I realised I'd never encountered anyone like Bob – he was the strangest and scariest person I'd ever met. There was simply no way I was going to work there, not with him, even though the job was mine if I wanted it. I decided to stay in Wagga until I felt 100 per cent fit.

When I got home I told my father that the interview had gone okay, but as for that Radford bloke … well, he was pretty strange. Dad said that Neil Maxwell had spoken highly of Radford, so maybe I'd get used to him, although he did admit that, on the strength of my version of the day, it sounded pretty awful. I told Dad that I wasn't yet fit and I thought I might stay on at the Leagues Club. He understood that, but felt that if I could recover my fitness and play in Sydney, I'd have a good chance of making the state side more quickly. Within a month I realised he was right, so I moved up to Sydney and started working for the amazing Mr Radford.

My main duty in my new job at the NSWCA was to appoint the umpires for each grade round – but more importantly, I suppose, I had to make sure that Bob's glass was never empty. He had two ways of letting me know that it was time for his first drink. We had an intercom system so he'd buzz me in my office and when I picked up the phone, all I'd hear were these ice cubes being tinkled in a glass. This was Bob's first sign that he was thirsty. His other method was a little less subtle. He'd buzz me and when I answered he'd call out 'Arse!' at the top of his voice. There was one time when he called out and I was busy elsewhere, and a few minutes passed without my bringing his drink. So he rang the intercom again and as soon as I picked it up he bellowed 'Fucking arse!' I got the message – and the drink.

But Bob was a true character. He'd spend his long, long lunches with such people as Michael Parkinson, the English cricketing twins Alec and Eric Bedser, rugby star Nick Farr-Jones and many other great achievers. After lunch, he'd bring them back to the NSWCA's boardroom, where I'd fix them drinks. Just meeting these people (and serving their drinks) was an incredible experience, a real education for me. Michael Bevan also ended up working at the NSWCA for a while, in the coaching and development area – and thankfully he was able to take on some of my barman load!

● ④ ●

Meanwhile, a handful of Sydney grade clubs had asked me to join them. Eventually I decided on the University of New South Wales (UNSW). There were a few reasons for this. The first was that I'd got to know Geoff Lawson, who played for the club when not turning out for NSW or Australia. Not only was he a fellow Wagga native, but 'Henry', as he was known, was the NSW skipper at the time and a stalwart of the UNSW Cricket Club. He had already been very encouraging to me. We'd first met at that training camp in Narrabeen a few years earlier, where he'd been a guest coach. And I'd always followed his career via the pages of Wagga's *Daily Advertiser*.

By the time I reached Sydney, I found out that Geoff had been keeping an eye on my progress, too. Henry always impressed me — I remember having lunch with him once, and looking on as he ate a meal of lettuce and tomatoes. His attitude to diet and his real commitment to fitness made me start to consider health and fitness much more seriously than I ever had before. Also, although I'd been known as 'Slats' for as long as I could remember, Geoff gave me my only other nickname — Sybil. He christened me one night in the bar of the University of New South Wales, after I got onto the stage and started singing with the band after a few beers with Geoff and some other blokes. Geoff decided that I must have dozens of different personalities inside me (and the more I drank the more personalities would emerge) — just like the character possessed by sixteen personalities in the Sally Field movie *Sybil*, although I hadn't even heard of the movie before that night.

The University of New South Wales offered me a sports scholarship to take a course in applied science. I could major in coaching or sports administration and then do a Diploma of Education to qualify as a schoolteacher in physical education. I thought it was a good package, so I signed up.

Although I was now part of the UNSW Cricket Club and the job at the NSWCA was working out well, physically I was still a mess — I was only about 50 per cent fit, at best.

In addition to my back pain, my weird, lopsided walk was causing pain in my knees, and despite my diagnosis with AS, the doctors and physios had not found a treatment that helped. And because of my physical discomfort, I wasn't sleeping well and in the mornings I'd be tired, stiff and sore. It would still take me until lunchtime to loosen up enough to walk sort of properly. I was taking six Voltaren anti-inflammatory tablets a day – two in the morning, two at lunch and two in the evening – just to get on top of the soreness. This was really overdoing it, so I was in no condition to play cricket.

At times I wasn't sure if I'd ever play cricket again. I sometimes felt that the university course would be all that would come out of my move to Sydney. But then how would I finish my course on a sports scholarship if I wasn't playing cricket?

● ④ ●

During those first twelve months in Sydney I could have moved home at any stage. I hated Sydney. I felt way out of my natural environment and depth, I had the AS condition which was making me crook and depressed, and I had no social life. And as for Steph and me, even though we were talking about our future together, we were still in the middle of a long-distance relationship. We both came from old-fashioned families. There was no way she was coming to live with me in Sydney, at least not yet. And her job at Grace Bros meant a lot to her, so she didn't want to give that up. I lived for most of that first year in the Sydney beachside suburb of Coogee with the Second Grade captain, Peter Trimble, who fortunately was a great guy, and I became involved in my cricket club, training regularly even though I didn't play in the early games.

My job at NSWCA was fine, although the surrounds weren't that homely. The building in York Street was pretty rundown and was completely empty except for the Cricket Association offices. At level four, at the top of the stairs, there was a sign warning you not to go further because the area was full of asbestos. It all seemed such a long way from Wagga. I racked up some serious miles, especially in the off-season, running back to my comfort zone in Wagga. I'd usually talk Bob into letting me leave work early on Friday afternoon and then get back to Sydney late on Sunday night, just in time to catch some sleep before starting another tough week.

I was very lonely in Sydney and ended up almost moving in with 'Henry' Lawson and his wife Julie at their home in Coogee. I'd eat there two or three times a week and they were really good to me at a time when I badly needed support. Henry was about the only person outside my family in whom I'd confided regarding my AS. I feared some kind of retribution if the selectors knew that I wasn't fit – I didn't want to be seen as a risk and I certainly didn't want to be seen as a guy who would use his injuries as an excuse for not performing. Henry had been in the same situation with a serious back injury and knew that I needed support and encouragement.

Besides keeping me fed, Henry put me onto his chiropractor in Sydney. He also referred me to Noel Patterson, another Wagga native, now based in Perth, who had helped Henry through his back injury. Noel was a top-notch chiropractor and was determined to find a treatment that would work for me. He gave me some information on AS and put me on a swimming program to strengthen my spine, so I'd drag myself off to the pool at the Sydney Football Stadium at 6.30 am for an hour, and I'd often go back for another session in the afternoon.

Yet in spite of all this treatment, I didn't seem to be improving enough to play First Grade. Eventually it reached a point where I thought I either had to play as best I could – or go home. Looking back, I'm surprised I actually stayed in Sydney. I was pretty down at the time, and with good reason. I had no close friends apart from the Lawsons and the guys at UNSW Cricket Club, I felt lost in the big city and I was in constant pain. And the whole purpose of my move – to make my way in NSW cricket – had stalled. Things were pretty grim. I spent a lot of time on the phone back to Wagga, talking to Stephanie or my father.

But I wasn't alone in taking this huge step to an unknown city. When you look at the course of Australian cricket history you see that many players, probably half, have come from the country. Contemporaries of mine, such as Mark Taylor, had made it through this huge change to the city. And such legends as Doug Walters had also made the shift from the country to the city. Doug, who came from Dungog, north of Sydney, was a gifted middle-order batsman who represented Australia in the 1960s and '70s, the kind of aggressive player who could change a team's fortunes with one great innings. But there were just as many country guys with real talent who either couldn't handle the move to the city or simply never tried it.

In the end it was my deep-down mental toughness and the desire to move my cricket forward that got me through. I decided I couldn't give up everything I'd established in Sydney, so I told UNSW that I'd play the next match if they wanted to pick me, even though I'd missed the first few rounds of the 1990/91 season. I lived in fear of that old cliché, 'If you don't use it, you lose it.'

Getting back on the cricket field helped me beat my blues and I began to feel a little better physically. But my movements were still so restricted that I struggled with the bat and running between the wickets was very difficult — and I was next to useless in the field. The morning after a match I'd feel awful and I was still knocking back six Voltaren a day. But slowly things were starting to improve.

●④●

I eventually got through the 1990/91 season with the UNSW Cricket Club and was chosen in the NSW squad for the next summer, mainly on the strength of a century I made in early January, which I followed with an innings of 75 the following day. By that time I was actually able to run, which mightn't sound like much but it allowed me to work on my general fitness and to take part in squad training, where I got to know the guys.

Then I experienced another key moment in my cricket career. The training squad was broken into four groups: north, south, east and west. I was in the same group as

Mike Whitney, Greg Matthews and Henry Lawson. They were the big guns. They were all Test players, guys I'd seen playing on television and had heard so much about. I really admired them and it was a great thrill to be in the squad with them.

While 'Whit' and Henry might've been the two oldest guys in the team, they were very, very fit. We used to go on a run from the Sydney Cricket Ground, up and down a few sets of stairs, then on to Centennial Park and back to the ground. I'd be close to Henry and Whit for most of the run. But then, with about 500 metres to go, they would put on a sprint and surge away from the rest of us. I'd be in that second pack: not fully fit but getting there.

After one run I came in about 30 seconds behind Whit. He pulled me aside and told me I should be doing better. He asked me how old I was. When I told him I was twenty, he reminded me that he was 32.

'You should be wiping the floor with us old guys,' Whit told me. And he warned me to watch out if he ever beat me again on the run.

Mike Whitney was a very popular character, a funny bloke and a natural entertainer (as his subsequent television career has proved). But he was also an incredibly committed, tough competitor. Whit was pushing me and I realise now what great leadership skills he was exercising.

What Whit said about fitness really made me think. I was impressed that he'd targeted me and was setting even higher standards for me than I had set myself. I think he saw a young guy who was starry-eyed about being in the state squad – and he also recognised that I was hungry for success. From then on, I'd listen to every word uttered by Whit and the other senior players, trying to pick up hints about how to improve my game. Coming from junior and country cricket – even at the highest levels – it's a big change when suddenly you're mixing with guys who've played for Australia.

On our next run I was nervous as hell, knowing I had to improve or I might lose this guy's respect. I managed to finish a nose in front of him – and I never lost to him again. It was another important lesson for me. Up to that point I'd had serious doubts about whether I could survive the training and show my peers that I deserved to be there alongside them. It reminded me that I actually had a fair bit of mental strength and, on a more practical level, it showed that the hard work in the pool and the gym was paying off. Maybe I really was ready for the big time.

Prior to the start of the 1991/92 season, we had a camp at Homebush where I actually won the main fitness test. The players congratulated me, and Whit and Henry in particular came over to tell me how well I'd done and how pleased they were that they'd finally found a young guy who was trying to show the way. That day, an hour after the beep test (which measures your oxygen capacity), I couldn't move a muscle – but at last I'd done well. I knew now that if I had to do something that really pushed me, I'd be able to manage.

With my confidence boosted I began to play regularly for UNSW Cricket Club, but it was in a few representative games I played for NSW in the Sheffield Shield that I did really well. When I made a good hundred in a Second XI game in Newcastle, former Test opener Rick McCosker came over at the end of the day's play to say how much he had enjoyed my innings. He said he thought that I had what it took to go all the way.

When I made a double century against the Academy at North Sydney Oval, I was beginning to believe I could truly make the grade. During this key season for my cricket career my guide was Michael Bevan, who was then in his second season of first-class cricket for NSW. We'd talk often and I'd ask him about state cricket and whether he thought I was good enough to make it. He gave me some good technical advice and was always supportive.

Towards the end of the 1991/92 season, after those two good innings in Newcastle and North Sydney, there were whispers that the state selectors were considering me. I thought my chance might come early the following season – but I was chosen to make my debut in the second last match of that same season. It was an amazingly satisfying feeling to tick that goal off my list.

I didn't do anything special in my first game in Hobart, but in the next match I made 60-odd against Western Australia in Sydney. I opened the batting and had to face Terry Alderman, who although past his prime was still an exceptional outswing bowler. My movement at the crease had improved a lot and I knew that I could play very attacking shots when I was seeing the ball well. Another dodgy year had ended really well for me.

To top it off, I spent a couple of months during the off-season in England, as part of an exchange program between the MCC and the NSW Cricket Association. As well as having the thrill of working at the hallowed Lord's ground as an administrative assistant, I also played a few games for the MCC. One was in Ireland, where I didn't score many runs, but I made a good hundred against Cambridge. I also got a 60 and a 70 playing in a game for Hertfordshire. That exposure to UK pitches would turn out to be extremely useful.

● ④ ●

By the start of the 1992/93 season, NSW were back at full strength. The squad included the Waugh twins and Mark Taylor, so I only came into the squad for the second game of the season, and even then only as twelfth man. But once the Test players got the call-up to play for Australia, I moved into the NSW XI, replacing Mark Taylor – and I played every game for the rest of the season. My movements at the crease were improving all the time, my shot selection was solid, and I had the confidence of knowing that I had a range of attacking shots with which to take on the bowlers. This approach was based, as it had been from my boyhood, on a sound technique and quick footwork. My AS was still giving me trouble, but now I was learning to live with it and had a solid program in place to help me stay on top of it. The other huge bonus about playing for NSW, for me, was the NSW team physio Patrick Farhart. He was my saviour countless times during my career, helping to keep me on the paddock.

I also learned a few lessons about batting along the way. In one game against Queensland in Sydney, fast bowler

Greg Rowell gave me two short balls, very early on, as a way of saying hello and checking out whether I could handle his aggressive, intimidating pace bowling. Dad had always said I should forget about the hook and pull shots until I was really set in an innings. Although I can't recall my Wagga coach Warren Smith telling me not to play these shots, he'd always recommended a 'risk-free' start to an innings. But on this day I whacked both Rowell's short balls to the fence.

When Dad and I spoke later on after the game, he'd obviously had a change of heart. He said that if I was able to play the hook and pull like that, I should back myself and go for it. I knew those attacking shots add greatly to an opening batsman's armoury because they make the fast bowlers realise you are not easily intimidated by short stuff. So my instincts were taking over, which meant there was no hesitation in my reactions. That's how you'd like to play every innings. The game doesn't work like that too often, but I certainly enjoyed my golden summer.

Two factors helped me build my confidence and develop the kind of attacking game for which I was becoming known. First, the NSW team environment was strong. The team leaders were prepared to back their players, even up-and-comers like me. As batsmen, we were given the freedom to play our own games – and that worked in my favour. In a different team a young new player might have been told to cool it, to hold back. To be honest, this wouldn't have come as a great shock, because I was opening with one of the most attacking batsmen in the country: Steve Small. Batting with Small was the other factor that contributed to my growing confidence that season.

'Jack' Small, as he was known, was so aggressive that anything I did at the other end just didn't compare. Yet opening with Jack was great for my game and we quickly developed a successful combination. We shared the same attitude to batting. As we reached the middle to start an innings we'd start growling at each other, saying things like: 'Yeah, let's kill 'em. Let's get stuck into these blokes.' We'd really rev each other up.

I realised later on, when I started opening the batting with Mark Taylor, that not everyone is like Steve Small. But he was a good partner for me at the start of my career because his aggressive attitude gave me real momentum. Before I knew it, I was playing a great number of shots and making good runs at Sheffield Shield level. I scored a maiden first-class century in my season opener against Tasmania at Hobart's Bellerive Oval in late November 1992. I continued to bat well throughout the season, backing my century with some solid scores and three further centuries. And although I didn't realise it at the time, the national selectors were taking note.

Other than the benefits of opening with Small, the rest of my first full season of Sheffield Shield cricket was a bit of a blur. When I look back now and compare my career then with that of opening batsman Matthew Hayden, I realise how different our paths were. At the time Matty was the other young gun in Australian batting and had scored 1000 runs each domestic season for a few years, but he'd struggled to break into the Test team. There wasn't much more he could do at state level. Then suddenly I appeared and would soon slip through into the top Australian XI. I'm sure at times he must have thought the world was against him.

Whereas Matty gradually developed a strong belief in his game and realised he could do consistently well at Test level, I came into Test cricket suddenly, after only a dozen first-class matches. So at times I lacked confidence in the depth of my game. I had come on in cricket so quickly that at various stages I had to prove to myself that I could do it, without the backing of a long track record. It's hard enough to prove to the selectors and the public that you can perform — it's even harder to do that if you have to prove it to yourself as well. And I'd never experienced a slump at first-class level, so I didn't know how to get myself out of one when it came.

I'd played a dozen first-class games, made runs against former Test bowler Carl Rackemann and Terry Alderman, both great cricketers, and basically thought that this first-class cricket was great fun. But I hadn't been forced to analyse my game in any depth. Of course that also had its advantages, because it meant I was playing instinctively, with a freedom that made me fearless. This approach had got me to the fringes of the Test team in just one year, so it wasn't all bad. But later, when some things went wrong after my first few years of Test cricket, I didn't know how to fix them — I just didn't know my game, yet. That was the downside.

But all that analysis was in the future. The present was

still rushing at me. At the end of the 1992/93 season there was all the usual speculation about the Ashes squad, for the forthcoming Test series to be played in England from May 1993. I was being mentioned, but I didn't give myself a genuine chance. I certainly wouldn't have bet on me. And even though I'd read a few columns from people such as Dennis Lillee and Geoff Lawson that mentioned me as a 'dark horse' contender, I chose to play them down. I didn't want to build up my hopes just to be disappointed if my name didn't make the list. I thought I was a good chance for the next Ashes tour, but not this one. No way.

Not long after arriving at the NSWCA office on 2 April, the morning the team was to be announced, I was buzzed by Bob Radford.

'Come into my office, young fella,' he barked down the intercom line.

My immediate thought was *What if he's about to tell me I'm in the squad?* I knew that a media release was sent out a couple of hours before the official announcement of the Test side. In fact, I'd even been tempted to hang around the fax machine and intercept the press release before it got to Bob. But I couldn't bring myself to do it, because I didn't want to be let down.

So my mind was racing when I sat down in Bob's office. I could see that he had the press release, and as I looked over I thought I could read the name 'Slater' upside down. Bob started going on with all this stuff that I wasn't that interested in hearing, and then suddenly he said: 'You're in. You're in the fucking squad. Ring whoever you need to and then we're going to lunch.'

Bob never needed much of an excuse to have a good lunch, and on this day he was genuinely excited. So we went out and celebrated my selection before it was publicly announced. Bob was knocking back the drinks, but I just had a couple of light beers. All I could think about was how close I'd come to not moving to Sydney, to staying in Wagga where life was easy and predictable and safe. It was ridiculous to think how near I'd been to missing out on this huge moment and opportunity in my life.

By the time we got back to the office two hours later, the team had been announced and the media were waiting. The rest of the day – which included my first, impromptu press conference in the library – raced by. I knew that Bob was absolutely delighted by my selection and by having been the one to tell me in person. But I didn't know what lay ahead and how selection on an Ashes tour would change my life.

When I gradually started to return to some kind of reality, it dawned on me that I'd never even played alongside or against some of the legends – Allan Border, Ian Healy, David Boon, Merv Hughes – whom I was about to call my team-mates.

Then something else smacked me right between the eyes. When I received all the paperwork that came with the selection, I discovered that my finances had also undergone a radical change in fortune. I think I'd been on $16,000 a year at the NSW Cricket Association as an administrative officer-cum-Radford barman. Now I was an Australian Test player, about to go to England on the greatest tour of all, with a lump sum of about $40,000 — and even more if we won the Ashes series.

It was all completely unfathomable to me. Where could I go from here? Where would this journey take me?

Chapter 5

Blaze of Glory

1993–1994

How did I feel about being selected for an Ashes tour after only one full season of first-class cricket? It was like being hit by a hurricane. There can't be too many other ways in which your life can change so suddenly – and so positively. After all the physical pain and personal confusion I'd been through, I had the feeling that someone up there really liked me after all. And even though I'd dreamed about this for years, there was really nothing and no one that could've prepared me for the hype, the thrills and the sheer intensity of the experience of Ashes Test cricket.

Admittedly, England had struggled to match Australia in Test cricket since Allan Border's side had won back the old urn in 1989, and star English players such as Ian Botham and David Gower were long gone. But neverthe-less, a full tour of the birthplace of the game still sits very high on the cricketing tree. That was certainly the case for me.

Typically, around Ashes time there's a lot of speculation before the selection of the squad and a lot of hype once it's chosen. There are photo shoots, interviews, congratulatory phone calls from family and friends. I went through all that in April 1993, but my head was in a spin – I hadn't had a lot of time to prepare for the experience and there wasn't much time to soak it up once my name was read out. The first thing I needed to sort out, however, had nothing to do with cricket – or at least not directly. The previous year Stephanie and I had become engaged and our planned wedding date fell right in the middle of the Ashes tour.

The marriage proposal had come about in a funny way. Although we were incredibly close, our decision to get married wasn't just romantic. My mother had recently moved to Sydney with her new husband Barry Smith, and she was running a hotel, which I moved into. It was the first time since she'd left us ten years earlier that Mum and I had the chance to spend some serious time together, so I stayed home a lot to be with Mum and didn't have much of a social life apart from when Steph was visiting. I thought: *Why not propose?* It seemed to be the logical next step, the sensible thing to do. It would bring us together. When we realised I wouldn't be in Australia for our planned wedding date, Steph was great, she was very understanding, and we put the wedding back a month. This was my first, but definitely not last, experience of how cricket at that level can impose on your personal life. I had no idea about the lifestyle of a top-level cricketer, no understanding of how that world can completely consume you. But I'd find out soon enough – and unfortunately, Steph would find out pretty quickly, too.

Just weeks after the announcement of the Test squad, I was on my way to Melbourne to hook up with the rest of the team, some of whom I'd never even met, let alone played with or against. In Melbourne I'd pick up my new Australian Test cricket gear, do some more media interviews and then board the plane for London. I was 23, engaged, and about to start on the greatest tour of my life. And I was in pretty good shape too, thanks to my new wonder drug Prednisone, which had helped me to fight off a bout of AS that had nearly forced me to pull out of the Ashes tour only the week before. (Prednisone had been prescribed by Dr Ken Crichton, a doctor who helped me enormously throughout my playing days.)

The shocks kept on coming. I arrived in Melbourne at about 10 pm on 22 April and when I checked into the hotel, the receptionist had a surprise for me.

'Mr Slater, here's your key,' she said. 'You'll be rooming with Mr Boon.'

My God ... David Boon, I thought. He was a legend, a true Australian sporting hero. We'd never met before and now I was going to be his roomy. As you can imagine, I was petrified as I went up to the room and knocked on the door (totally forgetting that I held a key to the room in my hand!). In any team you want to be accepted as a worthy member and I always seemed to feel this need more keenly than most. But who – and what – was behind that hotel door? How was everything going to pan out with Mr

Boon? After all, a member of the world-beating Australian cricket team and one of the best batsmen in the world was inside that room.

The man known universally as 'Boonie' came to the door with only a towel wrapped round him and a beer in his hand. He'd been watching TV in bed.

'You must be Michael,' he said, calmly as you'd like. 'Nice to meet you.'

That night we sat up until 3 am, having a few beers. Although I did ask a couple of questions, Boonie did most of the talking. He told me what to expect on an Ashes tour and reeled off some of his own experiences. In particular, we spoke about playing at the legendary Lord's ground and why it was the Mecca of all cricket grounds. It was an unbelievable night for me.

But all the while my official kit bag – known to players as 'the coffin' – was sitting in the room and I kept looking over at it. I was desperately keen to go through it and check out all my new gear. My baggy green cap was in there somewhere and I was dying to get it out. Eventually Boonie sensed my impatient curiosity and said, 'Go on, have a look at your gear.'

I was overwhelmed by how much equipment we received in our kit bag – it was better than Christmas! Although I had my own bats and gear, the coffin contained everything else I needed – tracksuits, shirts, shorts, even bike pants – and my Australian suit was hanging on a coat-peg nearby. When I finally found my baggy green, Boonie grabbed it and unofficially presented it to me, stressing that it really only means something after you've played your first Test for Australia.

That is the moment it *really*, properly, becomes yours. But I was so thrilled with my baggy green that the next day Boonie said he'd started to wonder if I'd go to bed wearing it! (I hadn't, I can assure you.)

Rooming with Boonie was a great experience and he made me feel as relaxed as I could in this wild, weird new world. Although Boonie was pretty laid back, I soon found out that he wasn't the best sleeper. Quite often I'd wake in the middle of the night and smell cigarette smoke. The room would be pitch black and all I could see would be the glowing end of his ciggie as he inhaled. The first time it happened I thought, *Wow, I didn't know Boonie was a smoker.*

For a new player like me, meeting someone like Allan Border, the legendary Captain Grumpy (or so the media led you to believe), was a pretty scary experience. Border was captain of Australia, a great player with a test average of over 50, and he had more determination and courage than the rest of us combined. AB was the ultimate in leading by example. He was someone you wanted to please – the kind of inspiring skipper for whom you'd play your guts out. Like all cricket-loving Australians, I knew that AB had been through some terrible times after he'd taken over the captaincy in 1985. But since then he'd worked amazingly hard, claiming the World Cup in 1987 and leading Australia to victory in the 1989 Ashes tour to England, despite going into the series as the underdog. Australia went on to retain the Ashes 3–0 in the 1990/91 series in Australia. In 1993, we had no plans to let him down by allowing England back into the contest.

AB was never a big talker at the best of times, but he made me feel fairly comfortable from the start. I recall my initial 'Hello'. I was just so nervous and overjoyed at the same time. It probably wouldn't have mattered how AB behaved, because I was always going to feel a little edgy until I had gone out and scored some runs for the team – ideally with that baggy green cap on my head.

Within a couple of days, after a few more promo duties in Melbourne, we took off for London. Owing to some kind of embarkation stuff-up, I was the last guy to get my boarding pass. We were all seated upstairs in business class, but instead of being next to Matty Hayden as planned, I was seated next to some guy who wasn't with the team. It didn't matter – on that first flight over with the Test squad, I was totally star-struck. I kept looking across the aisle thinking, *There's Boonie! There's AB!* It took a long time for me to settle down. Merv Hughes made our stopover in Singapore memorable – suddenly he came to life, sneaking up behind people at the airport and sneezing loudly, which scared the hell out of them. It was pretty funny at the time.

Arriving in London was awesome. The media were everywhere and there was so much hype. Everyone at Heathrow knew we were the Australian Test squad. Guys at customs told us that we were going to struggle. They said England had improved and they were going to regain the Ashes. But despite this kind of winding up, they all seemed really excited to have us in England. Having an Australian Ashes tour to England is always as thrilling for them as it is for us. And for this kid from Wagga on his first tour, it was an extra special time.

For three-and-a-half months we travelled through the UK on a massive touring bus, an enormous beast with 'XXXX' (the logo of our sponsor, Castlemaine XXXX beer) and 'Australian Cricket Team Ashes '93' plastered across its side. You couldn't miss us. Just like the bus, everything about the Ashes tour was bigger than I'd imagined.

The first thing we did when we reached our home base, the Westbury Hotel in London's salubrious Mayfair district, was to check in, dump our bags and head straight to a XXXX function. This was followed by a press conference, where AB introduced us one by one. Apart from AB and me, the players in that Ashes squad were Mark Taylor, David Boon, Mark Waugh, Steve Waugh, Ian Healy, Brendon Julian, Merv Hughes, Shane Warne, Craig McDermott, Damien Martyn, Matthew Hayden, Wayne Holdsworth, Paul Reiffel and Tim Zoehrer. I was quite nervous throughout all this. I felt like a little lost sheep, although you wouldn't think so by looking at me. I must have been quite a sight – I had a big smile spread permanently across my face and looked as though I was finding it hard to believe I was mixing with Test players. And of course I *was* finding it hard to believe, although the NSW players in the squad were great allies who made me feel comfortable and welcome.

During that first stay at the Westbury, I roomed with Queensland wicket keeper Ian Healy. Heals and I got on really well from the start – so well, in fact, that he became my room-mate on most tours. He also became my best mate in the years I played cricket. Although Heals wasn't an overly sensitive kind of guy and could be pretty tough on the field, our personalities complemented each other and we enjoyed the same things about the game: we played hard, trained hard and celebrated hard. Somehow we just clicked. It was almost like rooming with a brother.

● ⑤ ●

I may have been in the Ashes squad but I was no certainty for the Test team. I knew that, and the lead-up to the matches had been tricky for me. I was aware that Matty Hayden had the inside running for the vacant opening bat position alongside Mark Taylor, now that former opener Boonie had moved to bat at number three and Geoff 'Swampy' Marsh was out of the team. Our coach, Bob Simpson, had told me early on not to expect to play many games in England. I was just happy to be there, so I accepted his cautioning quite readily.

I'd been a huge admirer of Bob Simpson. His comeback to Test cricket at the age of 40, to help fill the huge hole left in the Test team by World Series Cricket, had been amazing. 'Simmo' had retired following the 1967/68 series against India, after more than ten years in the Test team. He'd also captained Australia 39 times and had a great record as an opening batsman, scoring almost 5000 runs, with an incredible top score of 311. Simmo had been out of the game at Test level for ten years when Kerry Packer's World Series Cricket split the international cricket world in 1977. Suddenly there was no 'official' Test team – all the best players had signed with World Series. So Simpson bravely came out of retirement and led Australia for the next two series, until finally World Series was disbanded and the big stars of the game returned to play regular Test cricket. In 1993, Simmo was regarded as the man who had turned Australian cricket around, especially from a coaching point of view.

Simmo had an interesting way of introducing himself to the younger, less experienced guys on tour. The team was given a few Peugeots to drive while we were in the UK and Simmo would drive one of them while most of us travelled on the bus. Early in the tour particularly, Simmo would ask a player, usually one of the new guys, to travel with him as a way of getting to know him and to explain what was expected of him.

When my turn came, Simmo told me that the tour would be a great learning experience for me, and that I'd play in the matches between the Tests but I'd struggle to break into the top XI. This was fair enough. I appreciated his honesty and it actually eased the pressure on me. I then felt I could enjoy the tour and play as well as I could during my limited opportunities. I would soak everything up, watch and learn in the dressing room and the nets, and generally continue my education in international cricket. The chat with Simmo helped me to settle in, and he remained a great support for me on my first tour. He knew a lot about batting and seemed to warm to me. And I think he respected the fact that I was prepared to work hard in the nets.

Matty Hayden didn't play particularly well in the one-day series that preceded the Tests, and he struggled a little in the three-day matches against the various county sides. I didn't do much better. I was twelfth man for the tour game at Worcester — but even failed as a drinks waiter. The 'twelfthie' has certain duties apart from mixing the drinks, such as finding new gear if a batsmen needs something replaced and generally helping out. I'd hardly done the job before, so I wasn't sure of the drill. At one point, Merv Hughes told me I wasn't pulling my weight and that upset me a bit. During that Worcester match I began to feel as if I wasn't fitting into the team very well. I knew that I had to prove myself, and the growing pressure meant that I wasn't batting well in the nets, the only place I could impress my new team-mates. As so often happened when I was feeling pressure to perform, I began to give myself a hard time.

Then, during the game, Simmo said, 'Right, Slats. Let's have a net.' Merv, who wasn't playing at Worcester either, came along to bowl. He obviously wanted to give me a going over because he went really hard at me, coming off his full run and bowling fast and aggressively.

To those who knew him well as a player, Merv Hughes was a smart, professional cricketer who knew his game, contrary to his public image as a wild man and a throwback to the beer-swilling, larrikin days of the 1970s. When Merv wasn't playing or when he thought he needed some solid work, he'd put in a huge effort in the nets. And that's what he did with me that day. I suspect it may have been another part of Simmo's plan to see what sort of person and player I was.

Bob Simpson wasn't the kind of guy to leave much to chance. I'm sure he had a word to Merv before this particular net session, telling him to give me the full treatment.

Simmo always emphasised the need to make practice sessions interesting and challenging. He taught us to work on all aspects of our game, to practise as if we were in the middle with fieldsmen under our noses, and to train hard. On a tour like this you practise in the nets most days and if you're not careful, the repetition can dull the brain and you drift into bad habits. Simmo was forever watching out for that.

This torrid net session with Merv was exactly what I needed. It shook me out of a flat patch. Once I'd faced a few balls, I knew Merv was having a real go. An event like this can turn around a season or a tour – it certainly did for me. With Merv tearing in at me I batted really well and proved to him, to Simmo and to myself that I could play well against one of the best bowlers in the world. At the end of the session I could tell that Merv was impressed, and his attitude to me changed after that. It was a sort of initiation, which I'd passed. I'll always be grateful to Merv and Simmo for those 40 minutes in the nets because they set me on the path to making my Test debut a few weeks later.

It also helped that I made 120 in the next game, at Taunton in Somerset, in a three-day match that began on 8 May, against an English side that included Test bowler Andy Caddick. It was my first innings for Australia in a first-class match – so in a sense I made a hundred on debut in the baggy green cap. It was a technically strong innings, and on that solid foundation I played shots that shocked even me. I realised I was playing on a higher emotional level than usual – and I now know that when that happened, I played at my best. I was riding the crest of a wave. I felt great.

I kept my form going and all I was concerned about in those early tour games was making runs. About two games before the first Test, Matty Hayden was rested and I made 60 in tough conditions. In addition to this, the successes I'd enjoyed while batting on English pitches in mid 1992 stood me in good stead.

I think AB was impressed and seriously started to wonder whether I should open in the first Test. Matty and I opened in the last lead-up game at Leicester on 29–31 May, in an informal, unspoken play-off for the Test spot. I'm sure we both felt the competition between us, even though we didn't speak about it directly. Neither of us wanted the other guy to fail, but within myself I knew I wanted to score more runs than he did – and I'm sure he felt the same about me.

This is an ongoing drama within the Australian team, the same today as it was in 1993. Because of the remarkable depth of talent in Australian cricket, every time you play for the Test team, you're also trying either to establish or preserve your place in the XI. As soon as you fail, there are always plenty of other equally strong players waiting for their chance to impress. Australian cricketers have the team ethic instilled in them from early on, but cricket remains an individual's game in many respects.

The emphasis on scoring and the extensive reference to statistics exacerbates this, because it makes it easy to quantify and isolate a player's performance. Computer-age technology exaggerates it still further. A defender in any football code could be the best player on the ground, but his performance can be overlooked. If an attacking player scores a few tries or kicks a goal or two, his efforts will always be noticed first and often he'll get the nod or the accolades as the best player on the paddock. In cricket every player's performances are measured and recorded on the score sheet – and because of this you can't help but feel the pressure as an individual, especially when you are vying for a spot in the team with one or two close rivals. And yet at the same time you've been trained to support your team-mates. It was a tough balancing act between selfishness and team spirit to play cricket for Australia, as typified by my rivalry with Matty for the position of opening bat.

During that final lead-up to the First Test, we played Leicestershire on a lousy pitch. I made 91 in the first innings (a sign of things to come as I developed a tendency to get out in the 90s!), and 50 not out in the second innings as we chased quick runs. Matty failed in that match. I'm sure my 91 proved to AB that I could grind out a score in tough conditions, and also blast away when needed.

Soon after, we were in Manchester preparing for the First Test. At the team meeting at the hotel where the First Test XI was to be announced, I happened to be sitting near Bob Simpson and AB, and I could see AB's notes. As he started talking about how difficult the selection had been, his arm was covering the sheet of paper with the list of Test players, so I couldn't read the names. Then he leaned back so that for about three seconds I could read the list – and I was sure I saw my name, just after Mark Taylor's. Then I got really jittery. Had I actually seen 'M. Slater'? Thirty seconds later, when AB called out my name, I wanted to leap out of my seat and scream 'YEAH!' at the top of my lungs. Instead, I just sat there in an excited daze, unable to hear any of the other names he was reading out.

I soon learned that the other members of my first Test XI, along with captain AB, were: Mark Taylor, David Boon, Mark Waugh, Steve Waugh, Ian Healy, Brendon Julian, Merv Hughes, Shane Warne and Craig McDermott. There was a team dinner after the meeting and that was when the real high started. I was in the Australian Test team and I was about to make my debut at the famous Old Trafford ground in the heart of Lancashire, my father's home county. Even though my rise to the Test team had been rapid, to me it seemed that I'd taken a lifetime to get there.

When I returned to my room after the announcement and team dinner, I immediately called Stephanie to tell her the great news and asked if she could relay the news to my family. I felt a sense of relief having spoken to Steph, and I tried to relax and drift off to sleep. This proved close to impossible given the excitement and anticipation running through my system. What would tomorrow bring?

● ⑤ ●

I couldn't have dreamed of a better debut Test series. I played all six Tests, averaging in the low 40s. I made 58 on debut at Old Trafford and 27 in damp conditions in the second innings. (It was during that game at Old Trafford that Shane Warne famously bowled experienced batsman

Mike Gatting with his opening delivery.) In the Second Test at Lord's I made my first Test century and scored 152 in the memorable innings described earlier. Simply to play at Lord's, the home of cricket, was an extraordinary experience. But to score a century in my first game there and have my name engraved on the Honours Board along with every other century and five-wicket haul ever made there … well, that was indescribable.

I'd already had an opportunity to soak up the atmosphere of this legendary home of cricket. During my two months helping out in the MCC office, I'd often stroll through the Long Room and stare at all the portraits and paintings of immortal past players. There is a feeling in the Long Room that is indescribable, a warmth and an almost tangible presence – perhaps the ghost of the legendary nineteenth-century English cricketer W.G. Grace! In 1992 the people I worked with at the MCC would say they hoped to see me back there the following year for the Ashes tour. I'd laugh and reply: 'Well, hopefully in '97.' To be back there so soon was some amazing turnaround.

A lot of people speak about the aura that surrounds the home of cricket – and it's true. Australian fans have told me they got goose bumps the first time they walked into the place, just for a tour. The place oozes history and just about every great cricketer there ever was has played there. To play my second Test there was like living out a dream.

Entering Lord's is like walking into a cricketing church. The ground has a special feel, a spirit all its own, and its own unique smell, which must have something to do with all that old wood. You can smell the age, the history of the place. Even practising at Lord's before a Test match is somehow different. I loved the nets there – at what they call the Nursery End, the opposite end from the famous Long Room – and the trip to the nets is memorable in itself, because you have to walk the length of the ground from the dressing rooms to the Nursery. It's an incredible place.

I felt indestructible after that 152 at Lord's in June 1993. My confidence was sky-high, life couldn't get any better – and I celebrated my innings and the Lord's Test in big style. After the game we had a huge party in a pub in Mayfair and I went way too hard. By nine o'clock I was outside throwing my heart up. But Boonie came and saved me. He ended up feeding me pints of water for the rest of the night until I recovered. What a guy!

That followed many hours spent in the rooms after the game, a time I'd really come to enjoy: we'd have a few beers, someone would crank up the ghetto blaster and then Boonie would sing the team song 'Under the Southern Cross'. When Boonie got up to sing it was a fantastic moment – we'd gather around him, link arms and scream out the team song until we were bright red in the face. Even the quieter guys in the team would get completely into it. Nowadays Justin Langer leads the team song after Test matches – and recently, in New Zealand in early 2005, I was invited into the rooms after a Test victory and discovered that the singing is as loud and passionate as ever.

That Second Test at Lord's was just incredible: I'd made a century, we'd won the Test and I'd even met the Queen after the game. And I'd only had to bat once, because the first three batsmen – myself, Tubby and Boonie – had all got hundreds and we'd won by an innings. On top of that feat, my room-mate at the time, Mark Waugh, had got 99. We later learned that just for a laugh an MCC member had made a £100 bet that the first four Australian batsmen at the Lord's Test would each get a hundred. The odds were about 1000 to 1. You should've seen the look on Mark Waugh's face when he found out, given he's such a renowned punter. I think he really felt for the guy who'd come within one run of winning that unlikely bet.

I was on such a high during that magic Lord's Test that when Steph arrived for a two-week visit in the middle of it all we had some trouble connecting again. The team policy for partners took quite a hard line: wives and girlfriends were allowed to come on tour but they couldn't stay at the team hotel, they couldn't even walk into the hotel foyer. Allan Border had introduced this strict policy during the 1989 Ashes tour. He'd had a gutful of losing and decided there'd be no parties in the team hotel and no mixing with the opposition team. But if the team won, then girlfriends and wives were welcome at the end of the tour. For Border, the team and the Ashes were everything.

When Steph arrived in London we hadn't seen each other for a while, and I guess it's fair to say that I was starting to change a bit. I was now totally engulfed in my new life in international cricket. I'd met some famous people and discovered that women were attracted to what I did – there was almost a rock 'n' roll element to it all. And I was starting to understand, and love, life in the spotlight.

Cricket and the lifestyle that went with it were like a drug for me. I was totally addicted.

The visit was a nightmare for both of us. Steph could see the changes in me and we had a couple of rows. She said that I was selfishly wrapped up in this world – and she was right. I was like a pig in shit, to be completely honest. To me, it was as if nothing else and no one else existed. I really didn't give her the attention I should have and she noticed it. I'm sure that if I'd gone on that tour without being engaged to Steph, it would have had a major bearing on the immediate future of our relationship. I'd entered a crazy, out-there world and it was having a real effect on me. It was an incredible period of growth in my life, for better or worse.

We were going to be married soon after I returned to Australia, but already I was asking myself, without saying it out loud, how this new life was going to affect our relationship. I had some doubts, not strong ones, but they were there, just under the surface. Were we rushing into things?

This was the beginning of the most exciting period of my life, but I was questioning whether everything – and not just our planned marriage – was happening too quickly. Maybe it would've been better for me to have slowly, gradually worked my way through the ranks, rather than race to the top after barely a dozen first-class games. In the space of three years I'd gone from the Australian Cricket Academy to struggling at grade cricket (due to my health), then to the NSW Second XI, the NSW state team and now the Australian Test side.

The rest of the Ashes series was thrilling, but it didn't quite match the Lord's Test. I didn't perform as well in the final couple of Tests, mainly, I think, because I was mentally fatigued. I'd put so much into those early games that my form just fell away.

Once I returned home to Wagga, I was back on cloud nine. In early September, Mark Taylor and I were given a tickertape parade and a civic reception in the park, right in the middle of town. There we were, putt-putting down the main street of Wagga in an old Rolls-Royce soft-top that belonged to the mayor. It was a fantastic day. I was treated like a superstar and I lapped it up.

The whole experience was surreal – and I began to realise how quickly things could change. It was over-whelming, and scary in a way too. I knew I now had to live up to all this, because people were suddenly looking up to me. In no time at all I'd become a sort of role model. What was equally weird was that I knew half the people who were waving at Mark and me as we cruised past in the Rolls. Only twelve months earlier I'd been one of them.

Some weeks later, on 14 October 1993, Stephanie and I got married at St Andrew's Presbyterian Church, in Wagga Wagga. This was another huge event in our home town. It didn't occur to us to organise security – it happened way before people thought about security for events like that – and we totally underestimated the interest in the wedding. When Steph reached the altar, she told me that she could hardly get into the church because there were so many people blocking the way. It felt like the whole of Wagga had turned out to have a sticky beak.

A lot of fellow state and Test players turned up at our wedding: Geoff Lawson was there, so was Mike Whitney,

Mark Waugh, Steve Small, Tubby Taylor, Wayne Holdsworth and Adam Gilchrist. My best man was my mate Neville Jolliffe, and my groomsmen were another mate, David Bell, my brother Mark and Stephanie's brother Paul. We didn't have a huge bucks' night, just a few beers the night before and a game of golf the next morning.

After golf, we all got changed at Dad's place, while Stephanie got ready at her folks' place. I was doing fine until I put the suit on – and then it was like Lord's all over again, but even more nervy. I sweated up a storm, worrying whether I'd get the vows out right and everything else.

When we came out of the church after the service, we nearly fell over backwards, because there were hundreds of people out there – and our wedding was a big deal in the local paper for days afterwards. I think they even sold photos to some big weekly magazines, there was so much interest in the event.

We had our reception for about 120 guests in the restaurant in Wagga's botanic gardens. It turned out to be a really great night. I didn't feel any of the uncertainties I'd been feeling about the wedding leading up to the big day, although perhaps deep down I just didn't want to think about it too much. I'd made a commitment, everything was organised, and we went ahead with it. And Stephanie soaked it all up, so it was a really happy experience for both of us.

We even scored a ride back to our hotel in a police car, with the siren wailing, thanks to someone Stephanie knew. On the way back, Steph told me a funny story. While she and her bridesmaids were getting ready, they noticed a lady sitting in the lounge room of her parents' place, quietly eating a sandwich. Gradually, people started to ask each other, 'Who's that? Who *is* that?' No one knew. It turned out that she was a local who'd just wandered in to check out all the wedding preparations. Our lives had really become very strange.

If only our honeymoon had been as great as our wedding day. I'd won the prestigious NSW Cricketer of the Year award for the past season, and the prize was a holiday at a resort in Coffs Harbour, on the NSW north coast – so we had our honeymoon there. But first Steph got seasick on a whale-watching cruise and then, just as she recovered, I got food poisoning. It was a bit of a disaster, really.

● ⑤ ●

My first home season as a Test player, which began in November 1993, was just as big as my Ashes tour. Up until the 1993/94 season, I'd always watched the summer tests on TV, but now I was out there in the middle, playing for Australia. By this time Stephanie and I had moved to Sydney. We rented a place in Randwick, in Sydney's eastern suburbs, for the first twelve months and then we bought our first home just around the corner in Queens Park. Owning a house was a fantastic feeling, I really felt as if I were part of something. Later on, in 1996, we sold that house to Greg Chappell and bought a large four-bedroom place in the same neighbourhood. We made the front page of the local paper at the time, because it was the highest price ever paid for a house in Queens Park – $805,000 –

which says as much about Sydney real estate as it does about my lifestyle in those days!

I played really well during that home summer, although the season had been tough, especially towards the end when South Africa won the Sydney Test. Fortunately, we'd won the First Test in Adelaide and drew the series. It was a 'split' series, with three Tests against New Zealand and then three against South Africa. I really consolidated my spot in the team that summer: I scored 99 in the second innings of the First Test in Perth against the Kiwis and followed that up with 168. I then scored 92 against South Africa in Sydney and followed that up with a solid 53 in the last Test in Adelaide. I scored just under 500 runs for the summer.

At the same time, Steph was starting to understand how it felt to be a 'cricket widow'. During the season I'd be travelling a lot and I was unsettled, totally wrapped up in the lifestyle. In many ways it's an unhealthy way to live – you're known everywhere and it can be very hard on a relationship. The issues and problems we had later on had a lot to do with the life I was leading as a Test cricketer. When I was home for any reasonable stretch of time it would take me a week or so to readjust to a normal routine. Once I'd settled down, our time together would be fantastic – but then another season would start up and bang, I'd be away again.

Although things were still good at that time, Steph would sometimes say, 'You don't seem like the Mick I went to school with anymore.' Maybe she was right. Cricket had begun to dictate my life, and Mick from school had moved into a whole new world.

Drinks Break

Tubby

I'd known about Mark Taylor since I was a teenager. I'd made it a point of finding out about the Wagga boys who'd gone on to do well at cricket, like Mark and Geoff Lawson. Mark is about five or six years older than me and during my early days with the NSW side it was hard to get time with him because he was usually away with the Australian squad. But of course his absence helped me out as well, because it gave me the chance to open for the NSW XI with Steve Small. When Mark and I did eventually connect, we got on well and built a good relationship. I guess it had a lot to do with that country thing, the Wagga link — it put us more at ease with each other.

Over the years we became really good friends on and off the field — we still are. Tubby and I have a great rapport and I think that's vital for an opening combination, you need to enjoy each other's company. That's what you see now with the partnership between Matthew Hayden and Justin Langer.

We didn't start off so well, though. I remember when we first met, just after my accident when I was at the Australian Cricket Academy. Mark came down to Adelaide with the NSW team to play against South Australia. The NSW contingent of the Academy was invited to spend time with the Blues (as the

NSW state side was known), and we sat in the dressing room with them during their match against SA at the Adelaide Oval. In the lead-up to the game we had a training session together and Mark hit us a few catches. I recall him getting frustrated with us, particularly with me, because whenever he hit the ball to my left side I couldn't catch it, due to my restricted movements. Towards the end of the session he asked, 'Don't you guys practise catching?' He told us we looked like beginners. Coming from one of Australia's best slips catchers, that really hurt.

I felt upset – not offended, mind you, just upset – because his comment was mainly directed at me, and I didn't want to offer what would've sounded like an excuse. The criticism was especially tough coming from a guy I held in such high regard.

But things improved when we started batting together. In the centre, what really worked for us was our left-handed/right-handed combination. It really does upset the opposition bowlers when they're forced to bowl to that combination, because they have to change their line of attack all the time and can never settle properly into a bowling groove. A bowler might have been concentrating on a particular ball to me, but then I'd get a single and he'd have to change all over again to bowl to Mark. I really think that interruption in the bowling increased the number of bad balls we faced per over, which we were then able to take advantage of.

I think our batting styles complemented each other, too. I was the more naturally aggressive player, whereas Mark liked to work the ball around. But on his day, he really started to open up, particularly towards the end of our opening partnership when we'd gained some confidence and momentum in our batting together. I think the fact that Mark was batting with someone more aggressive sometimes encouraged him to play bigger shots.

But one thing we did do quite differently was prepare ourselves for an innings. I didn't get ready to bat in a hurry — I was usually the guy who needed reminding when an innings was due to start. I found that if I was ready to go before then, it gave me too much scope to start thinking negatively. So I'd try to keep myself busy and in a positive frame of mind. The time for me to focus on my innings was when I walked out of the dressing room and onto the ground. But Mark was always ready quite early. He'd have everything organised and would concentrate on what he had to do, whereas I'd be laughing and joking and belting out a Bon Jovi song. We were complete opposites in that respect.

Tubby might say otherwise, but I think we generally had a good understanding when running between the wickets, despite the fact that we had three or four run-outs in the years from 1993 to 1999 when we opened the Australian batting together (excluding the time I was dropped from the Test side). I'd get a bit jittery at the start of an innings and would sometimes play a shot on the run, making a call as I went — which I guess didn't always help. But once my innings had settled into a groove my calling tended to become a lot more accurate. I also really trusted Mark's point of view and his calling of runs.

The one run-out I do remember was during the first Ashes Test at the Gabba in late November 1994, Mark's first home Ashes series as captain. We'd got off to a really good start, batting right through to lunch. I think Mark was on 50 or 60 and we'd put on more than 100 runs by that stage. Just after lunch he hit one straight to mid-on and called me through straightaway. This took me by surprise, because I sensed that the ball had gone directly to the fielder, which turned out to be the case. I called 'No' and didn't run. I remember feeling so bad when Mark got run out; I felt as though I'd spoiled the rock-solid understanding we had at the crease. I recall making a promise that I had to make a big score for Mark, to make amends for the bad call — and I did. I made 176 in that innings.

When we batted together, Mark could have a very calming influence on me. Certainly during the first half of my career I was incredibly competitive, maybe too much so. It was just me against the bowler. Mark and I would always talk between overs, and although he wasn't overly chatty, he'd tell me to take it easy and that would usually work — even though I'm sure he thought it went in one ear and out the other. His more placid approach to batting seemed to work well with my more upbeat, in-your-face attitude. And that same dynamic extended through into our friendship, despite our six-year age difference.

As a captain, Mark was quite different from Allan Border, whom he'd replaced when the latter retired in April 1994. I'd played my first fifteen Tests under AB, and I always felt that there was a big difference between Border as a person and as a captain. Off field AB was pretty happy-go-lucky, someone with whom I got on well, but as a captain he was quite intense and known for getting grumpy. I could see how the pressure from the press and certain other people affected him. In 1994 the first Australian tour of South Africa following the end of apartheid was one of the most memorable tours I ever went on, but by the end I could see that AB had had an absolute gutful of all the questions about when he was planning to retire. It was tough to see this great cricketer turn into Captain Cranky, wondering why the media wouldn't leave him alone.

Drinks Break: Tubby

I noticed that when Tubby took over as captain he did change, albeit slightly, and he made himself a little scarcer. It was a natural change though, one I'm sure every individual goes through when given the added pressure of captaining the Australian cricket team. Tubby still socialised with his team-mates, but you could sense that he now carried an added air of responsibility. Mark led by example and always played in a very professional manner, but he was still able to have a beer and a good time with the team and not let the pressure get to him too much.

Mark had awesome communication skills and could really read body language – I think that was one of the reasons he was such a good captain. He was always great with me, although he did pull me aside a couple of times when it was required. I remember one occasion when he quite rightly got into me. I'd been playing in the Australian side for about four years, and I was going through a period when I could get angry and be a bit precious about things – like accusing the Sydney Cricket Ground practice facilities of not being up to scratch after I got hit in the head by a ball. I put on a prima donna performance, storming off and actually having a go at the SCG groundsman, telling him that it just wasn't good enough. Mark let it go for a while, but then I had another dummy spit in Melbourne, during a fielding session. He lost it with me and told me to settle down and go back to being the person I was in the first few years of my Test career. He told me to get back to enjoying my cricket.

I think we had a beer that night and Mark admitted that he'd been watching me for a while and that it seemed to him as though I were frustrated all the time. Mark said that I wasn't the easy-going guy of a few years ago, who was out there because he loved the game.

'What's going on with you?' he asked. At the time I didn't think about it too much, but he was right. There *was* something wrong. That was the skill of Mark — he could identify problems and then pull you aside as both a captain and a mate and give you a chance to talk things over.

A funny story came out of our huge partnership at Lord's in June 1993. After I scored my hundred, Mark was still a few runs behind me, and I kept getting a lot of strike. Mark tells this story too, at speeches and lunches — and I think it's been embellished a bit. As he was approaching his hundred, I'd get a single off the fifth or sixth ball so I'd be up the other end to face the next over. My typical over that day might have run like this: defensive shot, four, two, defensive shot, dot ball, then a single. Mark started to get quite frustrated by the time he got into the 90s.

To be honest, I was aware of this — but I was in some special batting mode, I was enjoying it so much that I was oblivious to everything else going on, other than the run calling. When I got into this mood of feeling so good with the bat, I always wanted to hang on to the strike — not in a selfish manner, I just wanted to feel the bat on the ball. I always played at my best when I let my instincts take over, when I didn't think too much, and this was one of those occasions. I just couldn't drag myself away from the strike.

So, after a few overs of hogging the strike, I hit one off spinner Phil Tufnell down to long on and there was an easy single on offer, maybe even two runs. The calling of the run went like this:

Me: 'Yes, easy one.'

Tubby: 'NO, GO BACK!'

Me (three-quarters of the way down the pitch): 'Come on Tub, easy one.'

Tubby: 'NO! F***ing go back!'

I now had to run all the way back to the striker's end, and then the over was called. Between overs we had our regular chat and I asked Tubby what he was doing.

Me: 'Tub, there was an easy one there.'

Tubby: 'I know.'

Me: 'And this is Test cricket; every run should be taken.'

Tubby: 'I know. But Slats, if you look at the scoreboard, you'll see "M.J. Slater 144".'

Me: 'Yeah – I'm going great, aren't I?'

Tubby: 'Yes, you are. But if you look just below your name, you'll see that M.A. Taylor is on 96.'

Me: 'Shit, Tub, you only need four runs for a Test-match hundred at Lord's.'

Tubby: 'That's right. And for me to get from 96 to 100 I need to face a f***ing ball!'

This is the way Tubby relates the story. I'm not quite sure if it was as severe as that – but there is definitely a lot of truth in it. He eventually went on to get his hundred and it was a great occasion for us both. It was our second Test match together, we had a 250-run partnership, and I think this set the tone for our opening partnership over the next few years.

I was really at ease when I batted with Mark, and I think that was one of the reasons we batted so well together. Opening the batting for Australia was always such an extreme buzz for me, such an adrenalin charge. It was a great feeling to walk out there, particularly when I was batting with Mark, someone whom I respected so much.

Chapter 6

Runaway

1994–1995

Istill remember the tour to South Africa in February–March 1994 as one of the best of my career – as much for the hospitality and enthusiasm of the locals as the cricket itself. It was huge. We were the first official team to tour the country following the end of apartheid and we were treated like royalty. We were even formally introduced to Nelson Mandela at a private cricket ground belonging to a diamond millionaire where we were playing a game. Meeting Mandela was a great honour and I remember being struck by his wide-brimmed hat, which was just like the one Greg Chappell used to wear on the field. We visited some incredible parts of South Africa: we had a few days kicking back in Sun City and after the Durban Test we spent some time at a private game reserve north of the city. We were taken on trips to wineries, we played golf, and we attended special functions.

On the field I found the South African fans a lot like the Australian fans: tough but fair. Of course that South African tour is also known for the incident that occurred during the First Test at the Wanderers ground in Johannesburg, when Merv Hughes swung his bat at someone in the crowd. To get onto or off the Wanderers Ground you have to go through a 30-metre tunnel with the crowd on either side of you, and as Merv walked off after being dismissed, someone hurled some abuse his way. He responded by poking his bat in the guy's direction and ended up getting fined. But apart from that moment, I found the South African fans were above all thankful that they were involved in the world of international competitive cricket once again.

Some tours, like the 1994 South African trip, you remember for all the right reasons – you score heavily with the bat, the team plays some great cricket, you win the big matches – and then there are the tours that stick in your memory for other reasons altogether. My first trip to Pakistan, in September 1994, was one of the latter tours. The tour actually started in Sri Lanka, where we played a series of one-dayers. We played what was called the Singer World Series, starting with a game against Pakistan on 7 September, which we won by 28 runs. Following that we were beaten by India in a day–night game, when their master batsman Sachin Tendulkar scored a hundred. Finally, Sri Lanka beat us in a rain-affected game in Colombo. I got a couple of starts, a 26 and a 24, but only scored 54 runs in my three digs.

Despite the civil unrest that had broken out at the time,

Sri Lanka was a friendly place and I found the people to be always good-natured. It was as if they'd been born with a smile – which constantly amazed me, because they'd grown up with very little in the way of material comfort and they earned even less. But they loved cricket. Their eyes would light up if they got to meet you. We were treated like gods (and the subcontinent isn't a place where you can say that kind of thing lightly).

From there we headed to Pakistan for a series of Test matches and some more one-day games. It was a good series for me, especially when I scored 110 at Rawalpindi during the Second Test. But the results of those games are long forgotten, mainly because it was the tour on which a few of the Australian team were dragged into a gambling scandal. There had been whispers of this kind of thing during the Sri Lankan leg of the tour. During a match in Colombo against Pakistan we felt totally out of the game, yet Pakistan lost chasing our meagre total of somewhere around 150. We were incredibly proud of that victory – we thought we'd pulled off a really spectacular turnaround.

But early in the Pakistan tour we began to hear rumours that they'd thrown the game. I remember being completely shocked when I first heard that whisper. I just didn't understand. 'What do you mean the game was thrown?' I asked. Someone actually had to explain to me that the game had been fixed: because they didn't want to win they deliberately under-performed. This was completely new to a win-at-all-costs 24-year-old guy from the bush. Honestly, I nearly fell over – how could anyone wearing the Pakistani badge, presumably with all the same honour and pride I felt playing for Australia, possibly underachieve and lose a game for financial gain? It was later proved to be true, which was something way too large for someone like me, in my second year of international cricket, to understand. It was earth-shattering to think that this kind of thing could possibly happen.

The Australian players approached to throw some of the Pakistan one-day games were Tim May, Shane Warne and Mark Waugh. I think they were offered $US50,000, which was to be paid in a brown paper bag, of all things. I believe the offer was that Mark should score under 20, and Tim and Shane should serve up some juicy full tosses and half-trackers. Of course, as soon as they were made the offer, they contacted the Australian team management, letting them know what was going on. Certainly during my era – and I'm sure it's the same now – there was no one in the team who would get involved with this kind of corruption.

I was disgusted, totally deflated by the events of that tour. I was even more shocked when I found out that the South African batsman Hansie Cronje had been involved in something similar. When we'd toured South Africa earlier that year, Hansie had scored 200 against us in the First Test – but he'd gone straight to the nets afterwards because he wasn't happy with how he'd played. I remember thinking, *Wow, what dedication. What a work ethic.* So I just couldn't believe that Hansie had been involved in something which went completely against the spirit of the game he obviously cared for so much. It was devastating.

Mark Waugh and Shane Warne didn't know what they were involved in, but they were being sized up by the bookie to see if he could get them in more deeply. I guess that's what happened to Hansie. The chain of events leading up to the revelations about the Australian players is vividly etched in my mind. I was rooming with Mark Waugh, and as well as playing cricket I was doing some radio work with 2 Day FM in Sydney. I'd have a pre-match chat on air, talk about the playing conditions, the likely side, and whatever else was relevant to the game. This was something I ended up doing for a few years with 2 Day FM on pretty much every tour. It was a good grounding for the commentary work I'm doing today.

About half an hour after I placed my call to the radio station, Mark took a call and said almost exactly the same things as I'd said in my call, adding a few other details. He said the weather would be fine and the pitch would most likely take spin, so we'd probably play Tim May and Shane Warne. He also said that if we won the toss we'd most likely bat first. After Mark hung up, I asked him what radio station he was working for, because his discussion was so similar to mine.

He told me that it wasn't a radio station, it was an Indian fellow who called him and paid him US$1000 every time he spoke to him and passed on that kind of information. I thought nothing of it, apart from: *Wow, he's an experienced cricketer, he's been around – I hope someone will ask me to do that when I've been around for another couple of years.* The call seemed innocent enough, and a handy source of extra income. Later, it was revealed that Shane Warne had done the same – I think they were paid about US$9000 over a period of a few months.

Of course it was only a couple of months later that Mark learned he was speaking to the illegal bookie, Johnny Gupta. Mark didn't know that, he just saw the guy as someone who paid him a thousand dollars for giving over innocent information. A lot of us did radio work, just like my gig with 2 Day, and we'd provide that sort of stuff quite readily. It didn't take a mastermind to work out that pitches on the subcontinent would spin – and of course you'd take two spinners into the game if that were the case. And you only needed to open the window or read a newspaper to find out the weather report.

But following the whole Hansie Cronje drama, the South African match-fixing scandal that broke in 1998, it turned out that illegal gambling on cricket was a huge business – as much as hundreds of millions of dollars can be bet illegally on a single one-day game. There's a lot of money involved, and if a bookie has a player on side, well, the rewards must be huge.

● ⑥ ●

Fortunately my next overseas tour, to the West Indies in March–May 1995, stands out as one of the highlights of my career, and for all the right reasons. I'd been in top form prior to that. We'd thrashed England during the summer at home and I'd scored three tons – 176 in Brisbane in November 1994, 103 in Sydney, and 124 in the last Test in Perth in February 1995. I'd started fantastically well in that home season and my big hundred in Brisbane was the perfect beginning to my first Ashes tour at home. There were lots of runs made on both sides that summer, as Atherton and Thorpe scored really well for England.

I remember looking at the scoreboard during the Sydney Test – where all the aggregates for the series to date were shown on the screen – and seeing that I was level pegging with a few others. I decided, *I'm going to get to the top of that list by the end of the series*. And I did. I genuinely thought I had a chance of winning the International Cricketer of the Year award, a true honour, but Australian fast bowler Craig McDermott, who'd had a fantastic season (capturing 32 wickets in the series against England), won it by a narrow margin.

I got a century in the second innings in Sydney, where we had to fight hard for a draw, with the light fading. Then we went to Perth, where I got a lucky hundred – I was dropped two or three times – but I also had a feeling of great satisfaction, to be scoring runs on a quick, bouncing wicket with English paceman Devon Malcolm in the middle of the quickest spell of bowling I've ever faced. I ended up batting in the second innings with a broken thumb, thanks to Malcolm. But the series lived up to all my expectations.

We had a great time at the end of the Perth Test, too. English batsmen Mike Gatting and Graham Gooch had announced their retirement, and after we'd had our usual dressing room celebrations and team song, the English team came in and stayed on for hours. The game had ended early in the afternoon and we were still going at 6.30 or 7 pm that night. At one stage, Gooch had gone back to his hotel to raid his team's stash of Tetley's beer, which he brought back. It was a great night, even though Mark Taylor and Ian Healy, as captain and vice-captain – and who were both in the thick of it – were afterwards given a serve by management.

That night we had an official function and an appointment to get our inoculations for the upcoming West Indies tour. Needless to say, some of us missed out on our inoculation. As satisfying as this Ashes series had been for me and the team, the West Indies tour of 1995 still tops it in my book.

The 'Windies' had been dominating world cricket throughout the 1980s and it had been more than twenty years since Ian Chappell's Australian side had last won the Frank Worrell Trophy. We had our sights set on that trophy. It was like our Holy Grail.

From a discipline point of view, touring the West Indies could be hard at times because the temptations were everywhere. We were staying at resorts with holiday-makers, so there were pristine beaches, beautiful clear blue sea, swim-up bars in the pool and the whole calypso attitude. And West Indians have a funny understanding of time – they'd say five minutes, but five minutes could be an hour.

However, in 1995 we had a real will to succeed, a desire to beat them at home and bring back the Frank Worrell Trophy. From a batting point of view it was ridiculously hard, because such relentless fast bowlers as Curtly Ambrose and Courtney Walsh were coming at you all the time. They were incredibly intimidating. You'd try not to show the pain you felt but it was hard when your ribs were bruised and broken.

We didn't play very well in the one-day series that preceded the Tests. The team seemed to be out of sorts. Although I was one of the more consistent batsmen in the series, it just wasn't the start we had hoped for. So there was a bit of panic in the camp prior to the First Test in Bridgetown, Barbados, on 31 March–4 April.

First there'd been that period of transition, the changeover from the one-day squad to the Test team. The two sorts of cricket require vastly different batting styles. In the one-dayers, you tend to go for everything and try to build a score as quickly as possible; whereas in Test cricket you have time to get the feel for the pitch, the conditions and the bowling, and to build an innings gradually. And then there was the drama with our bowlers. Craig McDermott got injured and had to go home, Damien Fleming had a back injury (from memory) and headed off also, so Paul Reiffel and Brendon Julian were brought into the team. Frankly, we were in a bit of a mess.

For some reason things then began to change in the lead-up to the First Test. The white Test match outfits seemed to bring out a greater focus in everyone. Simmo trained us hard in this lead-up and by the time we got to the First Test, things just seemed to click and we won in grand style.

Mark Taylor and I had to go out in the second innings and get 40-odd runs to win. I distinctly recall that we said, 'Look, if we get these runs and we're still in, you grab the three stumps at one end and I'll grab the other three.' It's great to grab a stump and get a memento of the match – and there were some great performances in that game, which deserved some kind of keepsake. We were not out at the end of the game (Kennie Benjamin bowled a no ball that gave us the win) and we grabbed our three stumps each and started to run off. But then the huge crowd invaded the pitch. It seemed as if everyone in the whole place had run onto the ground, and all of a sudden someone behind me grabbed one of the stumps. It was gone in a flash.

I still had two stumps and I was hanging onto my bat, when suddenly a tug-of-war broke out between me and whomever was trying to grab the second stump – I ended up on the ground wrestling this guy. He didn't want my bat, he just wanted the stumps. So I finally got off with just one stump. And then I turned around to see where Mark was. He was going through the same drama as me. I saw Mark show his boot to some guy, effectively saying that he'd spike him if he didn't let go of the stumps Tubby had left in his hand. I think Mark ended up with two stumps, while I managed to hang on to one. It was almost as tough an experience as batting against pacemen Walsh and Ambrose.

We then lost the next match in record time, I think it was two days, in bad conditions in Trinidad. This was followed by a draw in Antigua, so it all came down to the last match in Kingston, Jamaica, which began on 29 April. I'll never forget that final Test, even though it had been a frustrating series for me. I was batting better than my statistics would indicate: I got a couple of good starts in Barbados; I got my first Test duck in Trinidad; I hit a very good 40 in Antigua and had a couple more starts in Kingston. Despite some good beginnings, I ended up scoring only 140 or so runs in the series.

So we had to beat them in Kingston. If it was another draw, the trophy stayed with the West Indies. That last Test was memorable for the extraordinary batting effort of the Waughs. Steve scored 200, Mark got 126, and between them they put together a huge partnership that helped win the game by an innings – and the series. Steve's fantastic double hundred in Jamaica was one of his many remarkable feats with the bat and summed up his great qualities: unbelievably heroic levels of grit, determination and concentration. That innings put Australia in a winning position, allowing us to win back the Frank Worrell Trophy after a decade of fierce, lost battles. We were completely euphoric that day, it was an incredible feeling.

Apart from our historic win, the really enjoyable part of that tour was a ten-day promotional stint to Bermuda. We played three one-dayers against the Bermudans, all for the good of the game. It was only a couple of hours' flight and it just rounded things off nicely after the Test series win. In fact, we kept the celebrations going from the West Indies all the way to Bermuda. I think Bermuda is just about the best place I've ever been to. All the houses were pastel colours, the water was almost too blue to be true and the sand was so fine and pure it was almost pink. It was a good time for us to reflect on our win and, as I said, to keep the celebrations going. All up, it was a tour to tell the grandkids about, that's for sure.

Chapter 7

Bad Medicine

1996

My first Test tour to India took placc in October–November 1996, but it was only for a one-off Test in Delhi, followed by a one-day tri-nation series against India and South Africa. I'm still surprised that there isn't more Test cricket between Australia and India, given our (relative) proximity and shared passion for the game. Although I do recall that the ground in Delhi was still being revamped at the time – and Indian grounds always seemed to be undergoing construction, which might be part of the problem.

A one-off Test can be very hard. That was especially the case with this Test, where the Border-Gavaskar Trophy was at stake, because we hadn't played a lot of cricket leading up to it, and I hadn't played any cricket in India before. (I'd been part of the 1996 World Cup tour team, of course, in February–March, but never got the call-up for the one-day squad.) One Test match isn't enough: you need at least three to play what I would consider a proper series. But unfortunately this was a one-off and we were beaten comprehensively. And even more unfortunately for me, the strongest memory I have of that Test is the shot I played in the second innings that got me out.

The match was played in typical Indian conditions: hot, dry and dusty. From the first morning there was no grass at all on the wicket, it was completely bare, and extremely conducive to spin. The wicket was always going to break up and take a lot of turn, but that's the way wickets generally are in India, as I found out.

In the first innings I top scored with 40-odd, having got out caught and bowled by Anil Kumble just after lunch. I was disappointed, because I thought we were going along nicely and I was definitely batting well – but then we had a big collapse. India had a bowler named David Johnson, who would steam in off a really long run-up. He ran faster than he bowled, but if he got it right he had the ability to bowl a quicker ball or two and an away swinger. But he was no major threat and I didn't feel intimidated by his bowling. As it turned out, in the second innings of the game I became his only Test wicket – and it wasn't in a style or circumstance that I remember fondly.

I hadn't scored when Johnson bowled me a very full, wayward ball that started wide and just kept going. I'm sure that if I had let it go it would have been called a wide – it barely made the pitch. But I had a huge rush of blood when I saw this ball, and thought to myself, *I can really belt this, I can smash it through the covers*. I didn't care if I hit it along the ground or over the top, because I thought there was no way anyone could stop it. But because the ball was so wide, I really had to stretch to reach it. Somehow I managed to top-edge the ball and it flew at incredible speed to first slip, where Mohammad Azharuddin, the Indian captain, was fielding. He jumped up and stuck out his right hand – and the pill stuck there. It was one of the most embarrassing dismissals I would ever have in Test cricket, an absolute shocker. I'd like to think that Azharuddin was the only fieldsman at that time capable of taking that catch, but it was still a lousy shot on my part.

My walk off the field was about the longest and loneliest I'd ever experienced. I trudged off slowly, knowing that because of the way I played the shot it would be replayed on a loop whenever anyone talked about our loss. It was a cow of a shot – and I felt very, very embarrassed when I saw the replay in the dressing room afterwards.

This shot, and the fact that we also lost the Test, upset some of our officials. The media also got stuck into me, suggesting that my technique had loosened up. That dismissal became the focus of all the attention on me at the time. For the next few days I was pursued by journos asking for a comment about it. But I ignored them: I had no plans to talk about the shot right away. Not long after, however, just before a training session, I finally decided it was best to talk it over with a couple of journalists. They asked me what was going through my head at the time and what I'd been thinking since I'd seen the replay.

'You know what? If I received that ball another nine times, I'd probably score 36 runs – this was a one-in-ten chance that I'd get out,' I replied. 'That's the way I play and it's unfortunate I got out but I'm going to continue playing that way because it's brought me a lot of success.' And I left it at that. It was a comment made out of frustration, as much as anything else.

It turned out that wasn't the sort of comment the selectors wanted to hear. I was subsequently dropped before the next home series against the West Indies, which ran from November 1996 to February 1997 – and I'm sure 'that shot', as well as that comment and the way it was received, were the catalysts for my dropping. I think what the selectors wanted to hear me say was: 'It was a mistake. It was a bad shot, I regret playing it and I certainly won't be playing another like that again.' But I suppose my ego was at work and I was annoyed by the fact that I was copping such a hard time about that one shot.

I think this is where my problems started with Geoff Marsh, who was the team coach at the time. Although we hadn't talked about the shot, I could feel that Swampy was frustrated with me. I later learned that he thought that I didn't listen. Marsh himself had been a cautious opening bat, a nicker and nudger, with a strong cover drive and cut shot. I think from around 50 Test matches he averaged just under 40. Marsh played a lot of one-day cricket in his day, but I don't think his conservative approach would suit the modern game if he were playing today.

In the few conversations I had with Marsh during training, I'd always get the feeling that he was trying to temper my game. He seemed to want me to play in a different style, more like the way he approached the game, and I didn't appreciate that. I rejected his advice because I wanted to stay true to myself and the way I played, not through pure stubbornness. The only change I could have really made was in tightening up my technique. I listened to Marsh, but at the same time I believed in my game. You get a lot of advice during your life, and I've learned that you have to filter out the good from the bad.

There seemed to be unspoken issues between Geoff and me. Perhaps we should have had a beer together and talked things through. In 1993, when I was first picked in the Australian side, I'd heard that there were two players who were upset at my selection: Dean Jones and Geoff Marsh. When I was picked – and especially after I'd made those runs in England that year – it effectively blocked Marsh's chance of returning to the Test team. The uneasiness that had grown between us made me wonder if he was still hanging on to that in some way.

Hindsight being the useful thing that it is, I now know that I should've spoken to Geoff about this. I should have cleared the air and found out exactly what he wanted from me, because it seemed to me at the time that everything I did on the field was frustrating for him – especially an incident in the one-day series that followed on from the Test match in Delhi.

● ➐ ●

My position in the one-day team was always less certain than my opening spot in the Test XI. I made my debut in the Australian one-day side during the 1993/94 summer after making some good runs in the Tests against New Zealand. I'd made a 99 in Perth – the first of nine 90s I'd make during my career – and 168 in the Second Test in Hobart.

It was a special thrill to make the one-day team. This was the more glamorous side of cricket, with the coloured clothing, the coloured pads, the crowds that behaved as though they were at a footy final – and finally I had a chance to play day/night cricket. When I was presented with my coloured gear I got just as big a thrill as when I first laid my hands on my baggy green that night in Melbourne with Boonie.

The first one-day game I played was against South Africa at the Melbourne Cricket Ground on 9 December 1993. It was an experience I'll never forget. I scored 73 off, I think, 69 balls, which remained my highest score in the 'pyjama' game. There were at least 70,000 people in the ground that day. The atmosphere was everything that I expected – and then some.

I really had a good time, playing some big shots. I remember hitting Hansie Cronje for six over extra cover and everyone in the southern stand just went crazy. It sent tingles down my spine, it was such a buzz. I got out trying to hit their spinner Pat Symcox out of the ground. The ball dropped on me a little bit and I was caught and bowled. I'd tried to hit the ball so hard that I'd actually badly pulled the tendons in the back of my hand, running into my wrist. As soon as I came into the sheds I iced my hand. But later on, while fielding, I dived to stop a ball and landed on my left arm. The pain was incredible.

Afterwards, I had to tell the physio that I was injured, but I played it down a bit, because I didn't want to miss the next match, which was only three days later, against New Zealand. I was just so excited about being in the one-day team. But it turned out to be a big mistake, not letting on how much I was hurt. I failed with the bat in the next game. By the time I came to play my third game, in Sydney on 14 December, my injury hadn't improved at all. That night at the SCG the ball was moving all over the place and South Africa's Fanie de Villiers got me out for 10. I was dropped for the next game.

I realise now I probably should've stepped down for a game to let my hand heal properly. But I didn't, and as a result my one-day career fell into what was to be an ongoing pattern: I was constantly in and out of the team. It didn't help my place in the one-day side that Bob Simpson thought one-day cricket might loosen up my technique – he didn't want my one-day play to make me overly aggressive in Test cricket. The one-day game was a source of constant frustration for me, because I knew I was good – and I was ready for this different type of cricket – but I wasn't given the chance to play a few games on the trot and cement my position.

I didn't play in the first couple of one-day games on that 1996 Indian tour, but I was picked to bat at number six in a game against South Africa, at Gauhati on 1 November. I got lucky. Star fieldsman Jonty Rhodes dropped me early and I ended up with 53 not out. We batted second in the following game at Chandigarh, against India. We were chasing a few runs when I came in, again at number six.

We were in such trouble that it looked as if we'd lose the game, but Michael Bevan and I locked into a great partnership – and suddenly we had a serious chance of winning. It was down to about 30 runs from 30 balls, but then Michael was bowled. The responsibility was now on me to get us through. I ended up getting out lbw, trying to whip one across the line. I made a half-century that day, but we lost the game by a few runs.

On the way back to the hotel we were all really disappointed. The loss meant we wouldn't make the final – and to have won that would have been some kind of consolation after losing the Test match. Later that night in the hotel, I greeted Geoff Marsh as he walked by. He didn't say anything until he'd gone about six feet past me. Then he turned around and replied:

'You're happy with yourself, aren't you?'

I didn't know what he was getting at. I turned and said, 'Excuse me?'

'You think you've done your job today, don't you?' he continued, adding that everything was all right for me because I'd scored another half-century.

'No,' I said. 'We lost. I'm *not* happy with that.'

I understood that Marsh was trying to secure his place as team coach, and he was under some pressure. But still I thought his comment was strange, especially coming from a coach, because he seemed to be suggesting that I placed my own performance above that of my team, which just wasn't true.

Bad Medicine

When I got back to Australia I spoke to Mark Taylor about my situation. I'd been out of the one-day team for some time but had since managed to score two half-centuries batting down the order, which was an unfamiliar position for me. I thought playing different positions in the two forms of cricket would be a good blend for my game: I'd open for the Test team and bat in the middle order for the one-dayers. Mark agreed and felt that my batting at six in the one-dayers would take the pressure off nicely. It seemed like the perfect balance to both of us. But at the time, there was a lot of talk in the media about the promotion of Victorian opener Matthew Elliott to the Test team. Elliott had had a sensational summer the year before and had started the summer of 1996/97 really well, which, potentially, was a bad sign for me.

Prior to the West Indies series, which was to begin on 22 November 1996, I had two first-class matches in which to make my claim for the Test team. The first was against Victoria, Elliott's team. Of course everyone started talking up the battle between Elliott and me for the opening spot. There was a lot of comparison of his solid technique with my technique, which most writers felt had developed a few flaws, especially after 'that shot' in Delhi.

Elliott made some runs in that lead-up game, and I got a 60 in the first innings. I remember Dean Jones (who was a very chatty guy on the field) saying things like, 'Ooh, you never know. Slats needs the runs here, Matthew Elliott's going to get picked.' But I still thought my 60 was a good result (even though I should have got a hundred), so I felt all right.

The last game before the Test series was to be played against Queensland at Bankstown Oval in Sydney. We batted first, and I started well, but I ended up being dismissed for 20-odd. While I was sitting there watching the middle order bat, I had a chat with Steve 'Brute' Bernard, the former NSW fast bowler. He was now an Australian selector; there was always a selector at each state game. I knew Steve pretty well from my time working with Bob Radford. He'd sometimes come in for a drink and I'd serve him. Steve asked me how things were going and I told him that although I hadn't made a score for a while, I was batting pretty well and felt that I was due for some runs. Brute told me I might as well save them up – the time to do it would be in the First Test against the West Indies, he said.

It seemed clear to me that Steve's comment implied there were no worries about my selection for the Test in Brisbane. Everything was good, I was still in the team. Given what the media were saying at the time – they were calling for my sacking – this made me feel pretty good. I was reassured that my spot in the team was safe and I could forget the newspaper talk. And my statistics seemed to back me up: by then I had played 34 Test matches on the trot and was averaging 47. I really felt that it was hard to question those sorts of figures.

As it turned out, I didn't get many runs in the second innings of that match against Queensland, but I kept in mind Steve Bernard's comment and didn't feel too threatened by another low score. When Queensland knocked off the few runs they needed to win on the last day, the loss hurt – but not as much as what unfolded prior to play. I was doing some stretches and sit-ups on the ground when I spotted Steve out of the corner of my eye. Next thing I knew he was right alongside me. It was then that I sensed something was wrong. I was already feeling defensive – even though I'd tried to stop reading the papers, there'd been a few more negative stories that day about me and my spot in the Test team.

Bernard told me that I'd been left out and Matthew Elliott had been picked. My response was one of spontaneous fury. I had absolutely no time to collect my thoughts and think about how I should take this terrible piece of news. My worst nightmare – being dropped from the Test team – was coming true.

I asked Steve what I'd done wrong. I also asked him why he was trying to manipulate players' careers – I really thought he'd worked me over by reassuring me that my spot in the team was safe. I stormed off the ground, shouting back over my shoulder that he was playing with my career. I realise that this was an irrational response, but it felt as though the guy had ripped out my heart. I guess I've never been especially good at hiding my feelings or directing blame.

When I got back to the dressing room, my NSW teammates clearly knew what had just happened. They tried to be sympathetic and console me, but I was in no mood for that. They then backed off and didn't speak to me. Stephanie was at Bankstown Oval that day, so immediately after the match I grabbed her and my gear and headed for my car. But a media scrum had already formed and there were loads of cameramen waiting to get a shot of Michael Slater, the newly dumped Australian opener. In all the flurry of activity and commotion, one of the cameramen nearly pushed Steph over just to get a shot of me. I was livid.

'Do that again and I'll thump you,' I snapped at the guy, and we finally cleared out.

Although I regret the way I handled the situation, I still feel incredibly disappointed by my dropping. I think it was really severe. In my whole cricketing life to that day nothing could have prepared me for the first time I was dropped from the Australian XI. At that stage the game was my life, my very heartbeat. It was everything I wanted to do. I also loved the lifestyle that came with it (fortunately, although out of the Test team I was still contracted to the ACB, on a slightly reduced figure, and could live comfortably). I think my severe reaction to being dropped may have backed the selectors into a corner – when Matthew Elliott was injured weeks later in the Sydney Test against the West Indies, the selectors picked Matthew Hayden to replace him. They couldn't back down and pick me. It would have looked as though they'd made the wrong decision in the first place.

I was never really given a clear explanation of why I was dropped, even though I tried to talk it through with Steve Bernard one day in the Royal Hotel in Randwick. Unfortunately, I didn't come away from that meeting any wiser. All I could gather was that they seemed a bit nervous about the way I was playing in the lead-up to the 1996/97 West Indies series, at the same time as all the talk going on about

Matthew Elliott's good technique – and it just blew up from there.

It's still one of the most disappointing times of my career.

Chapter 8

Keep the Faith

1997

It was a fairly lengthy road back to the Australian team for me, which probably wasn't helped by that outburst at Bankstown Oval just before the West Indies tour. My comeback spanned a period of about a year and a half, until March 1998. In the first six months alone, I missed two home series (the 1996/97 West Indies tour and a Carlton United Series between the West Indies, Pakistan and Australia) and a South African tour from February to April 1997, which was a major disappointment for me. I'd been on the 1994 tour to South Africa when we'd drawn the series, and I really wanted to be on a winning tour to South Africa. But that was not to be, and I never got to tour there again.

I'd also been dropped from the one-day team, too, soon after being dumped from the Test side. It seemed to me that Geoff Marsh had got his way, as I was sure he influenced my dropping. He tried to call me several times soon after, but I refused to take his calls – which, again, was not the smartest way to deal with the problem on my part. I just didn't want to talk to the guy whom I felt had master-minded it all.

I also felt there'd been a Victorian push at the time for Matthew Elliott. He was a classy player in good form and the Victorian media were really behind him – and sniped away at me whenever I gave them a chance through a low score.

As for Mark Taylor, he fell into the worst slump of his career when he started opening with Elliott (although that might be nothing more than a coincidence). Mark and I had worked up a really nice balance in our partnership and that changed when he opened with Matty Elliott.

It took me longer to get over my disappointment at this stage of my career. And this wasn't helped by people telling me that mine was one of the harshest sackings they'd ever seen – dropping someone with an average of 47 and all the rest. I felt a bitterness and anger that lingered for about six months.

When you're dropped, you also drift apart from the players in the Australian team. I've always said that being in the Australian team is like being on a freight train: when you're on it, you just keep motoring; if you fall off (when you get dropped or injured), the train just keeps rolling. All you can do is pick yourself up and scramble back on board in the best way you can. But I felt lonely out of the Australian side and I started to question the mateship within the team – and when you start sinking into those sorts of feelings, it's terrible. Only when I got back into the team did I realise that the selfishness is what is required to keep yourself in the team. But it's a huge shock when it first happens. I felt like my whole world had been taken away from me.

Stephanie was a great support while I was coming to terms with being dropped. When I was playing well I'd be on an incredible high, I'd be on top of the world. But if I made a low score or went through a lengthy slump, Stephanie would became the innocent victim. Like the partners of all sportspeople, I'm sure, cricketers' partners are sucked dry, their energy is sapped, by the highs and lows of sporting life. But by now Stephanie understood the lifestyle, the craziness, the unhealthiness of it all, and she had a good relationship with other cricketers' wives and girlfriends, like Sue Porter (Mark Waugh's partner at the time), Jane McGrath, Lynette Waugh and Helen Healy – they were a team in themselves. Through these friends Steph was more in touch with the team than I was. I think this understanding between the players' partners is steadier than that between the guys. The girls always had a strong support network, based on friendship beyond the pitch, so it was more real in a way.

As for me, I struggled for the most part during that summer of 1996/97 after being dropped. By the end of the domestic season I only averaged in the high 30s. But I did get two half-centuries in the Sheffield Shield season-ender against Tasmania, which NSW won after a big run chase in the last innings – and I think that was enough to convince the selectors that I should be back in the Ashes squad for the tour to England from May to August 1997.

Soon after that match against Tasmania, I had a call from the Australian Cricket Board to let me know that I'd been selected for the England tour. I was completely over-the-top happy. I probably should have kept it a bit more in perspective, but once you're out of the team all you want to do is get back in. And I felt that I'd made it back as quickly as I possibly could, especially given the controversy surrounding my dropping.

I remember how elated I felt getting into that seventeen-man squad. And I really thought I was a chance for the Test team, because Mark Taylor's slump had now spanned a few months. There was even talk about whether Mark should go over, but his brilliant captaincy and good relationship with the ACB kept him on track. But when he arrived in the UK, the tabloid press gave him hell. They'd even plant people behind him with three-foot wide bats, and take photos that they'd run with a headline saying this was what Taylor needed to get out of his slump. It was pretty harsh. Mark responded by scoring a century in the second innings of the First Test at Edgbaston in Birmingham – prior to that he was as good as gone.

Once Tubby got those runs, I knew it was unlikely that I'd play in a Test on that tour. I didn't wish Mark any ill will, because he was such a great team-mate and friend. But it was a strange time for me, especially going back to Lord's. The 1993 Test had been such a key moment for me – it was where I'd proved I could make it at this level. Not to be playing there on this tour was a bizarre experience. Although, admittedly, it did have some advantages: Lord's serves the best lunch in the world of cricket, so I was able to get stuck into the food during the Test. I must have gained about five kilos in those five days! At least I was there and part of another Ashes success, although I did feel some strong self-doubt about not making the first XI. I didn't feel as bulletproof as I once had.

I had a miserable time with the bat on that tour. It was a bit like my one-day career, or my experiences at those teenage cricket carnivals: every time I got a bat I was trying to prove to everyone that I was ready to go, and I simply tried too hard. And there was no regularity in my playing. I have a computer printout of that tour and the letters DNP – 'did not play' – appear almost everywhere by my name. I got 90-odd in a one-day game against Scotland and that was my tour highlight. Sometimes I'd go for a month without having a bat.

One bonus for me was that Steph came over for most of the tour and we had a wonderful time travelling around England. Steph had worked with Grace Bros until late 1995, but because we hardly saw each other between our two busy lives, we agreed that she should leave her job. Although, I then got dropped, and suddenly we were seeing too much of each other! Steph had such a good relationship with the people at Grace Bros that they welcomed her back. But when I returned to the team she gave up work for good. Given that in my peak I was earning between $400K and $500K a year, there was no financial need for her to keep working if she didn't want to.

When the Ashes tour ended, Steph and I took a seven-day cruise down the Nile and saw some of Egypt. I think it was the best experience I've ever had in my life, anywhere.

It was just fantastic. When we returned home I realised that the few months away had been a great experience and our relationship was in a really good place.

● ⑧ ●

I had a solid domestic summer in 1997/98, but I was still out of the Test team. I was batting well but feeling as though I just wasn't quite on top of my game – although it was easier than the previous summer.

It was a tough road back because I had trouble letting go of the anger and confusion I felt about being dropped. I now know you need to get over these emotions as quickly as possible. But it took six months before I was able to sit down and clearly plan a way back. Without a plan, it probably would have taken even longer to get back into the Aussie team. I think my return was accelerated because I took the time to see a sports psychologist. I'd been exposed to sports psychology since my time at the Australian Cricket Academy, and I've always been very open to the idea of the mental game and that sort of psychological stuff. Sports psychology really helped me out. I found it enabled me to clear my mind if I was getting a bit confused. But you have to make sure you find a psychologist you can relate to, as some can be a bit too technical.

What I learned was this: the danger is to think of the end result (being selected again) rather than breaking it down into the little steps you need to take to reach that end result. To stick with small steps makes a comeback more likely. It's just like scoring a century: if you start thinking about reaching 100 when you haven't even got off the mark, you'll never achieve it. But if you break a century down into batches of ten runs, then it becomes more manageable. You don't get too far ahead of yourself. So I wrote down all my thoughts and devised a plan for re-selection.

The steps I needed to take were pretty straightforward. With every training session, quality was the key – I had to practise in the same way that I wanted to bat out in the centre. From grade matches for UNSW upwards, I had to take advantage of any batting opportunity I was offered. I batted in increments of ten and my new mantra was simple: *Play quality cricket shots*. Whether it was a forward defence, a good leave or a quality pull, every shot had to be the best shot I could make. I needed consistency, and preparation was the key.

During that time I also had regular chats with my mentor and junior coach from Wagga days, Warren Smith. It's crucial to revisit the basics when the wheels fall off, and Warren really helped by reminding me not to get ahead of myself, telling me the things I should be doing and where my focus should be. The idea of not getting ahead of yourself was reinforced by a fellow called Laurie Lawrence – no, not the swimming coach – with whom I'd stayed during my Green Shield days. He told me how to break an innings down: when you get to 30, take guard again and start from scratch; do the same at 60, and so on; and always respect the good balls. My hard work paid off, because I came in for Matthew Elliott for the tour of the subcontinent in March 1998 (Elliott had been dropped when the Test team returned from South Africa in 1997).

This time I was more subdued when I was recalled. I'd been a little too excited by my recall for the 1997 Ashes tour – and this time I needed to make the runs. I knew this was my last chance and I really had to make it stick. We left for India in early 1998 and the First Test began on 6 March at Chennai. In the lead-up to the Test I got a 90-odd in a tour game in Mumbai. We then went to Vizag, in south-east India, where we played against a President's XI. I made a double century but was on the receiving end of a very dodgy lbw decision while batting against off-break bowler Harbhajan Singh. I was spewing – I actually came close to being cited for dissent. I was just so pumped up for that tour.

So I hit the Test series ready to go, but I missed out in both Chennai and Kolkata. I was now two Test matches into the three-Test series for the Border-Gavaskar Trophy. I was thinking, *Shit, I'm in trouble here*. I remember former Australian batsman Neil Harvey, who was sometimes good for a quote, popping up to say something along the lines of 'Oh, Michael Slater's got a dodgy technique.' I was feeling really pressured.

I knew I had to score runs in the last Test at Bangalore, which started on 25 March. I'd been feeling really intense during the first two Tests, staying in my hotel room a lot and probably training a little too hard. But I wasn't very disciplined in the nets and that flowed through into my game. So when I got to Bangalore, I made sure I didn't lock myself away in my room too much – and when I was off in my room, I'd write down my goals for the game. And each night I'd have a couple of beers with the guys.

Keep the Faith

I also had a change of heart about my cricket gear. I'd used Gray Nicolls bats for my whole career, but I realised the bats I'd brought to India were probably too light. In India the pitches play low and slow, so you hit the ball down the ground more and you need a heavier bat. I'd change the weight of my bat depending on where and who I was playing. Against the West Indies in Australia, I used light bats, because I played a lot of pull and cut shots against their fast bowlers. But on the subcontinent I used heavier bats because I played a lot of front-foot shots that required the extra weight. I realised I had really messed up by bringing these lighter bats.

I had a word about my bat quandary to Warnie, and he gave me an Indian-made Vampire bat, which Sachin Tendulkar had given him. (I didn't want to upset Gray Nicolls by playing with another bat, so I pulled the Vampire stickers off and replaced them with the Gray Nicolls insignia. I phoned Gray Nicolls to tell what I was doing because I felt guilty about it. It wasn't the done thing. Philosophically I didn't agree with it, but I was just so keen to get runs at this stage of the tour.) When I got into the nets at Bangalore, I revisited the work ethic that had served me so well up until then: I stuck to the basics and tried not to get out.

Clearly it worked. I got 91 off about 110 balls in the first innings and it felt great. My 42 in the second innings was really good, as well. My target for a Test match was always to score a total of 100 – or more. So I did that and felt I'd made a healthy contribution. And we won the Test as well (although India took the series). It was a huge event for me.

I remember leaving Bangalore the next day feeling incredibly relieved. I knew then that I'd be selected for the next tour, which was against Pakistan. I was now well on my way to securing my position in the Test team for the second time. I was back.

That's me, aged about three, on one of our school holiday adventures with the family. I was quite the beach baby.

Dad and me in the backyard of our house in 'Nappy Alley', on campus at the university. As with sport, it seems my passion for cars started early in life!

Holidaying at Cedar Lake on the Gold Coast. This was in January 1982, a year before Mum left.

The all-conquering Turvey Park hockey team of 1981, with my dad Peter as coach. My long-time mates from Wagga include Neville Jolliffe (*front row, second left*), David Bell (*middle row, fourth left*) and, in the back row, Geoffrey Cook (*second left*) and Andrew Sharrock (*far right*). I'm sitting in the middle next to Neville.

As part of the Riverina Zone XI (I'm at the front, second from the left), during the NSW U-17 Cricket Carnival in Dubbo. Warren Smith, on the far left, was my first coach and mentor.

This early '90s photo of Warren Smith and me was taken in a park near his home in Ashmont, Wagga Wagga. Throughout my career, Warren was the voice of wisdom.

NSW cricket legends Geoff Lawson and Mike Whitney both had a huge impact on my career – Geoff even gave me my other nickname, 'Sybil'. (Don't ask.)

This is me at the NSW Cricket Association office on 2 April 1993, just after being told I'd been selected for the 1993 Ashes squad. Out of shot, my boss Bob Radford was gearing up for another big lunch.

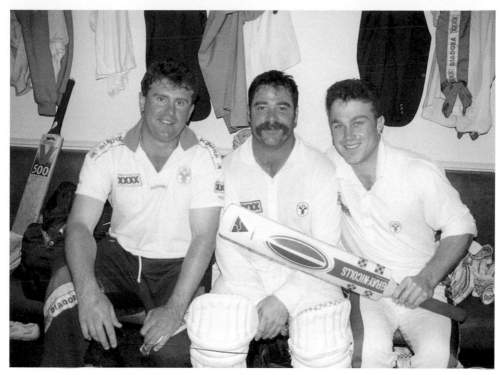

The stuff of dreams – a century at Lord's, and in just my second Test match. David Boon and Mark Taylor also helped themselves to hundreds in the same innings as we piled on the runs, declaring at 4 for 632.

On the balcony at Lord's, 22 June 1993, soaking up our Test victory. I was voted Man of the Match – fortunately Boonie helped me get through the celebrations in one piece!

TOP: Tubby and I create chaos as locals line Wagga's Bayliss Street to honour our Ashes triumph. Twelve months before this, I'd casually walk through town without any fuss. The change took some getting used to.

Stephanie and I on our big day, 15 October 1993. I'm pretty sure that the whole of Wagga turned up for a stickybeak outside St Andrew's Presbyterian Church.

My one and only Test wicket, playing against Pakistan at Rawalpindi in October 1994. Some say a fluke, I say a flawless in-ducking leg cutter. Waqar Younis isn't amused.

Trying to hang on to my souvenir stump – and my bat – after winning the First Test against the Windies, in Barbados, 2 April 1995. Facing Curtly Ambrose was never this tough …

Kingston, Jamaica, 2 May 1995. In the foreground, Boonie, Steve Waugh, Tubby, myself and Brendan Julian celebrate our series victory against the Windies – we were the first Aussie team to win there since 1973. It was a tough but incredibly rewarding tour.

The post-series party, this time alongside Justin Langer. Still proudly wearing our baggy greens, draped in the Aussie flag, and enjoying the moment with a couple of beers – it took some time for the enormity of our win to sink in.

On top of the world at the WACA, December 1995, after scoring 189 not out against Sri Lanka. Nothing beats starting the next day with a hundred already on the board. I eventually reached 219, my highest Test score.

Posing with the Channel 9 dream team at the Gabba, prior to a home series against the Poms. *Front row, from left to right:* Shane Warne, Ian Chappell, Richie Benaud, Mark Taylor, Steve Waugh; *back row:* Simon O'Donnell, Ian Botham, Tony Greig, Bill Lawry, Ian Healy and myself.

As a player, I needed to work incredibly hard to keep my fitness and stay on top of my arthritic condition. I always prided myself on being one of the fittest in the team.

Steph and I celebrate with a little tune after my reselection for the Test squad, before the 1997 Ashes campaign. The study in our Queens Park home housed all my cricket memorabilia and kept my spirits up while I was out of the team.

Pushing hard for a win in the 1999 New Year's Ashes Test at the SCG, Tubby and I put on more than 100 runs, but in the end we narrowly escaped with a draw.

A much-needed Test century at Wellington, in March 2000, against the Kiwis. Some fool on the hill with a megaphone heckled me throughout my 90s. I had the last laugh, scoring 143 – but it was my final Test ton.

How sweet it is. Savouring our opening-Test win against the West Indies at the Gabba, 25 November 2000. I batted well that summer, but it would be my last home season wearing the baggy green.

How sweet it is Part Two. I always dreamed of owning a Ferrari, and with a little help from a friend I was able to buy this baby in 2001. It was a big step up from my Ford Meteor.

This is from a festival game during the 2001 Ashes tour, my last trip with the Australian team. I always batted at my best when I trusted myself and remained instinctive. See the ball, hit the damn thing!

During my retirement lunch in November 2004, Jimmy Barnes and I reunited for the first time since my legendary cameo at the Allan Border Medal night some years before. 'Khe Sanh' again, this time without the glass of red.

My fiancée Jo and I getting some rays in the Maldives, December 2004, just after a commentary stint in India. Scary thing is, two weeks later, the tsunami tore this place apart.

An all-too-rare shot of me and my family (less my dad and stepmum) together in the one place. *From left to right:* Mark, his partner Nell, Carole, Barry, myself, Tracey (foreground), sister-in-law Cindy, Julian and brother-in-law Stephen. Family will always be the most important thing to me.

Dad and Claire were always there to help out, even during my darkest hours. This was taken on their wedding day, 21 August 1986.

Discussing the day's play during the 2004 ICC Trophy, for Sony TV. At times the commentary booth can be every bit as challenging – and fulfilling – as life out in the centre.

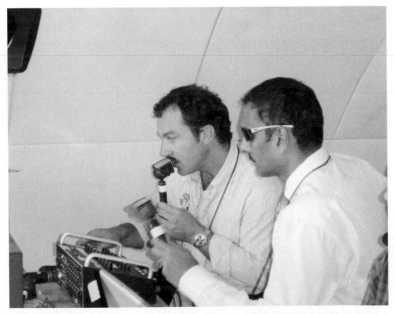

Alongside former Indian Test star Ravi Shastri, calling the England vs India NatWest Challenge match at Lord's, September 2004. Some of my most formidable opponents from my playing days are now my colleagues.

Chapter 9

Fear

1998–2001

It was good to work my way back into the side after being dropped from the Test team at the end of 1996 and reacting so badly to it. In the Test series in Pakistan in October 1998, following the tour to India, I scored well and began to feel my place in the team was more secure. It was following this Test series in Pakistan that I had one of my two major run-ins with Steve Waugh (the second was to come during the Ashes tour of 2001). After the Third Test in Karachi, the one-day team travelled to Bangladesh for an International Cricket Council (ICC) knockout comp, before returning to Pakistan for a one-day series. The Test captain, Mark Taylor, Justin Langer, Colin Miller and I were not in the one-day squad and we were heading our separate ways. So we had a night out, a final drink at the end of a successful Test tour.

We'd won the series in Pakistan 1–0, but it had been

particularly successful for Mark Taylor, who'd scored an amazing 334 not out at Rawalpindi, an innings that not only equalled Sir Donald Bradman's Australian Test record, but silenced a lot of critics who'd been saying Mark's best days were in the past. I'd done okay, too, scoring 108 in that Rawalpindi Test and another of my 90s in the Third Test in Karachi.

Because it was very hard to find places to drink alcohol in Pakistan, which is a 'dry' country under Islamic rule, we would often be invited to diplomatic places, such as the American Club or the International Club in Peshawar, or the British or Australian Clubs in Islamabad. All these places were permitted to have bars. So after a few drinks at the hotel we went to the International Club to kick on. At the time I was still upset by an article that a journalist from the *Herald Sun* in Melbourne, Ron Reid, had written about me after I'd got out for 96 in the Third Test. I felt I'd played really well, having top-scored in a first-innings total of 280. But after hitting off-spinner Arshad Khan for four down the ground I tried to repeat the dose to reach three figures off the next ball: I missed it and was stumped.

It was one of those rush-of-blood things that batsmen go through – perhaps it was something that Reid just didn't understand. I often wonder whether he'd have written anything if I had been dismissed for 86; there just seemed to be this stigma about getting out in the 90s. Someone at Cricket Australia would photocopy every article relating to the players and the team and fax them to the hotel. The team manager would then hand the stories around on the bus. Occasionally there'd be a big response if someone felt they'd been mistreated or misquoted. This was one of those cases.

Reid attacked me for playing an irresponsible shot. He gave me absolutely no credit for actually making 96 in the first place. No one in the team said much more than 'Bad luck, Slats.' When I read a fax of the article, I wasn't just disappointed, I was furious. I went up to the press area before the start of play the next day to speak to Reid. Because I'd had the night to think about how I was going to approach him, I was able to stay rational and calm, which allowed me to make my point clearly – something I wish I had done more of, rather than my usual aggressive, spontaneous responses! Reid backed down, admitting that while he thought it was a rash shot, the article was harsh.

But I couldn't let it go. Instead of leaving it at the ground, I started whingeing about it to the guys I was drinking with after the Test – Tubby, Langer and Miller, and others including Ricky Ponting, the Tasmanian batting star who would go on to captain Australia some five years later. I knew I was raving on a bit but somehow I couldn't help myself. Because I knew how hard I'd fought for that 96 when the team had been in trouble, Reid's article had cut deep. I had copped plenty from the press by this stage and should have dealt with it better. I think I felt it was purely another Victorian push to get Elliott back in the team, which I thought was out of line.

Before I cooled down, Ricky Ponting got sick of me talking about it. He turned to me and said, quite aggressively: 'Look Slats, we've heard enough about it. Would you just shut up? We're sick and tired of your whingeing about what Ron Reid wrote. Yes, it was unfair, and yes, you played well, but let it go.'

Ponting's comment caught me by surprise and, because I had a few drinks on board, I became angry. For 30 seconds or so we exchanged some pretty harsh words. Steve Waugh, who was in the group next to us and not involved in our conversation, came over and told me to settle down. 'Yeah, I'm sick of hearing you talk about it too,' he said to me.

That was way too much for me, especially because Steve wasn't part of the conversation, so I turned away from Ricky and started arguing with 'Tugga'.

'What the fuck are you getting involved in this conversation for?' I shouted at Steve.

It was the first shot in a very heated exchange. Now I'd had a slanging match with two of my team-mates. Not surprisingly, the night finished fairly soon after because of this clash and everyone thought it was time to go home. Steve went back to the hotel in a huff and I followed shortly after. I felt disappointed that it had happened, and angry that Steve had been involved.

Once I settled down, I realised what had happened: in short, I'd been drunk, irrational and silly. And I hadn't done myself any favours by talking as angrily as that to the vice-captain. I'd been fired up and it was a silly confrontation.

The one-day side was up and gone very early in the morning, so I didn't have a chance to have breakfast with Steve and apologise. But I knew they were coming back through Karachi again, so I wrote a letter of apology and asked the hotel liaison officer to hand it to him. I wanted to apologise for my aggressive (over)reaction. All Steve was trying to do was stop a scene between Ricky and me. Steve received my letter and sent me a text message a few days later saying, simply: 'Apology accepted.' It was a relief, but I still didn't quite understand why he'd got involved. I felt that we'd all – Ricky, Tugga and I – lost our tempers and overreacted. But I guess this can happen when you're living closely together for a couple of months in a strange country. The key is to be able to let it go and move on. Sometimes you can, sometimes it's harder.

● ⑨ ●

I really got among the runs in the home series against England in 1998/99. My place in the team was now very secure. During the home summer of 1999/2000, we played nine Tests – three each against Pakistan and India, and another three against New Zealand over the Tasman – and we won every single one of them.

I had a good run. I scored 169 in the First Test against Pakistan in Brisbane and 97 in the Second Test, followed by a 91 against India and 143 against the Kiwis in the Wellington Test. I scored almost 600 runs for the summer. It had been a busy stretch, from November 1999 to April 2000, and by the end of it I really needed a break.

My original plan was to spend three months at home doing pretty much nothing, but then I got a call from Gary Francis of Channel 4 in England. He asked if I was interested in going to the UK to do some commentating. Initially I wasn't so sure – I'd really been looking forward to the break. But I also knew it was a great opportunity, one that could lead to regular commentary work when I finally retired from playing. Steph agreed that it was an amazing opportunity and that a few months in London might be fun.

So, after a short deliberation, I called Gary back and said that I was interested in the offer. I'd only commentated a couple of times before, during two one-day matches in Perth in 1999. At that stage I was contracted to Channel 9 and working on *The Cricket Show*, which I really loved. I hosted various segments on the show, which ran during the lunch breaks of Test matches. I'd give batting tips, or do a news story about the Bradman Museum, or report on what new gear was on the market – that kind of thing. First I did it for a year 'on spec', and I'd get paid for each segment, but then I was contracted to Channel 9 from the second year onwards. I did this up until I was dropped from the team and it gave me a real taste for TV.

Apparently Channel 4 had become interested in hiring me after hearing my commentary that weekend in Perth in 1999. I didn't know that Gary Francis had been in the back of the box for one of my stints on air, and had liked what he'd heard. Mark Nicholas, the front man for Channel 4's coverage in England, had shared some time in the box with me. I'm sure that also helped my cause.

Gary explained that there was a shortlist of four people, including former English opener Geoff Boycott and my good mate Ian Healy, and he promised to get back to me quickly with a decision. Three days later I found out I'd got the nod, and Steph and I were off to England for four months so I could do my first proper stint of TV commentary.

I knew the necessary protocol, so before I agreed to the job I approached the ACB, who had no problems with the idea. This was a great career opportunity and I desperately wanted to make the most of it, although I did find that commentary brought on added pressure. I knew that Richie Benaud had done a similar thing early in his career, staying on in the UK after an Ashes tour, and that had turned out to be a brilliant move for him. Many decades later, he's still calling the game.

When I arrived in England, I realised what a brave new world UK TV was for me. My colleagues in England were Richie Benaud, the stylish Hampshire batsman Mark Nicholas, South African cricketer Barry Richards, spirited Warwickshire captain Dermot Reeve and West Indies cricketer Ian Bishop – all far more experienced commentators than me. After my first day on the job, in Nottingham, I was dismayed. I thought I'd had a shocker. Mind you, it wouldn't have mattered how well I'd done that day: all I wanted to do was impress everyone. Although I did get positive feedback about the work I was doing, it just didn't sink in. My perfectionism was rearing its head again.

After the day's play I went back to my hotel and got ready to meet some guys at a pub, but I really wasn't in the best mood for socialising. While I was giving myself a silent dressing down, the phone in my room rang. It was one of my colleagues. He had his guitar with him and asked if I wanted to pop in for a jam. We were both self-taught guitarists and while neither of us would cause Eric

Clapton to lose any sleep, we enjoyed mucking around with music after a day's work. So we got together and when I started to strum on his guitar, he pulled out a big joint and lit it up. He said it was 'good stuff'.

But he could have told me anything. I was clueless when it came to drugs. Apart from a few puffs of marijuana as a teenager I'd never smoked grass. Drugs had always been a big no-no for me. There'd been a few kids in my crowd growing up in Wagga who smoked regularly, but I certainly wasn't one of them. I thought cigarettes were definitely out and pot, to me, was several rungs below them. So to me 'good stuff' meant just that – it would be a pleasant experience. *Why not?* I figured. I wasn't playing cricket at the time, and my fitness wasn't an issue, and I was so annoyed about my start to commentating that I figured a puff or two might help me relax. Bad move.

My colleague had a number of puffs before handing the joint to me. I was a little apprehensive as I took hold of it, and only had two drags before giving it back. About five minutes later there was a knock at the door and in walked Mark Nicholas. He was taken aback by the smoke and the unmistakable, pungent smell of marijuana – and made it quite clear to both of us that he was surprised by what we were doing. He said we were being very unprofessional, a comment that made me feel really disappointed with myself. I mean, this bloke is the Richie Benaud of Channel 4 and he'd just busted me smoking a joint. Shit!

Then paranoia kicked in. Within a few minutes my body had gone numb and I could hardly speak. I was fighting these weird feelings as we left for the pub across the road where we were meeting a group of work and cricketing colleagues. I remember being in a group but speaking mainly to Paul Strang, the Zimbabwean leg-spinner. That was when I started to feel really awful. I knew I'd been hit hard and why I was feeling so bad, but it was a new and scary experience for me. I felt like I was on a slippery slope and everything seemed out of my control.

And it wasn't a mild attack. I started to feel queasy in the stomach and a bit strange in the limbs, but it was the paranoia that was overwhelming. It was a powerful and totally unfamiliar feeling. I became very anxious and had to get out of that pub, quick smart, and back to the hotel. My heart started to beat really fast and I bolted back to my room where I drank heaps of water and then lay down in the hope my heart would stop racing. It felt like it could burst through my chest at any second.

But I just couldn't calm down. Steph was visiting some friends in London, so she wasn't there to help me. I was really starting to lose it, so I ran back to the pub to ask this guy what the hell was in the joint. I thought something other than grass must've been used – no one had ever told me that a puff on a joint could do this to you. But he denied lacing it with anything. I could see his concern for me but it was too late to be of any help. Stupidly, I had done something that I'd never condoned and I was feeling so bad that I genuinely thought I was going to die.

Mark Nicholas noticed something wasn't right and came over to see why I was so distressed. I told him what had happened and that I was having chest pains and finding it hard to breathe. He immediately took me for a walk to try to settle me down. He assured me that it was only a reaction to what must have been especially potent grass. I was totally freaking out. I thought I was having a heart attack.

I was rushed to hospital with a pulse of more than 200 beats per minute. Eventually the incident was dismissed as medically unimportant – my problem had been psychological, not physical. The doctors said I was obviously stressed and had started hyperventilating and had then panicked. I was relieved by this diagnosis but still angry at myself for not having had the strength to say no to that joint. And I was embarrassed that it had happened while I was working for Channel 4. I really didn't want anyone to find out about it.

Later on, I learned that when my colleague had referred to 'good stuff', he'd meant that the marijuana was hydroponic – that it was grown under artificial light, which makes it much stronger than usual. Apparently, even regular dope smokers can find it hard to handle. For me this had been a totally overpowering, embarrassing and scary experience, and I vowed I would never touch any drugs – good stuff, bad stuff or any other kind of stuff – ever again.

While still in London, about a month later I had a similar attack, except this time I definitely hadn't been smoking any marijuana. I'd always felt that I was prone to anxiety, and it seemed the pressure I'd been putting on myself to do well in my new television role had brought on this second attack. I stayed overnight in a London hospital so the staff could run tests on my heart. All the results were normal, although a cardiologist did diagnose tachycardia, a slight flaw in the electric pulses of the heart that causes irregular beats. But in a majority of cases – mine included – it's not life threatening.

So what was I supposed to do? A specialist confidently gave me his verdict and prescribed heart medication, but my instincts were telling me something else. *He's wrong*, I thought as I left the hospital. *It's not my heart. But I'm not the doctor and I'm meant to trust his word.*

After the second episode in London, these attacks really started to kick in. I was soon having three or four a day and was even housebound for a couple of weeks, unable to go outside. Thank God that Steph was there with me for the entire summer, and her parents also came over. They all provided immeasurable support during a very tough time. Channel 4 was enormously understanding and gave me time to recover, which fortunately coincided with a few weeks during which there were no major matches. When I finally felt okay, I took on my next commentary gig in Kent, the county to the south-east of London. Mark Nicholas asked if I wanted to drive to Kent with him the day before so we could play a round of golf at the famous St Georges Club. I jumped at the chance, although I was nervous about leaving the safety of my apartment, just in case I had another attack.

The two-hour trip was uneventful until we were about a mile from the course. All of a sudden I felt waves of adrenalin pumping through my body and, once again, my heart started beating out of control. I thought, *Shit, here we go again* ... Thank goodness Mark knew the area well and quickly found a hospital. Given my heart and chest symptoms, I was rushed straight into the outpatient area for tests, which, as usual, confirmed that my heart was good as gold. So what the hell was going on?

The doctor looking after me that day was a young South African, only a year out of university. By now I was getting very used to the usual questions they'd ask me and I was waiting for the standard assessment, that they couldn't find anything medically wrong with me. But this doctor was different. He asked me a few extra questions and quizzed me about panic attacks. He said that he'd had a recent case almost identical to mine and that the person had been suffering from bad panic attacks, which at their worst mimic the physical symptoms of a heart attack.

Bingo! Diagnosis made by a first-year grad. I knew immediately that he was right. The challenge now was to get on top of the problem quickly, because I was in England to work and I wanted to make the best of the opportunity Channel 4 had given me. I really wanted to do the right thing by Gary Francis, Mark Nicholas and everyone else connected with the telecast. They'd all been very supportive.

It took another week or so to find a remedy and eventually I started taking an antidepressant (AD), not because I was depressed, but because this sort of AD had been shown to help control anxiety levels and prevent severe panic attacks. Three days later I felt much better and was back in the commentary box. And, most importantly, I was in a positive frame of mind.

Fear

I got through the rest of the season pretty well and I left England with some solid commentary experience. But I now had a nagging concern about being on antidepressants. I hated taking any form of medication – I'd had my fill of painkillers a few years back when my AS was at its worst – and I was worried what people might think about me if they found out I was taking antidepressants. Sure enough, my worries were confirmed. Soon after I returned to Australia word got around that I had a heart problem. Fortunately, the pills were working and I carried on with life quite comfortably, preparing myself for the upcoming home series against the West Indies in the summer of 2000/01.

● ⑨ ●

It's very difficult to explain a panic attack to anyone who hasn't had one. How about this: imagine impending doom is closing in on you and you feel like you're going to die. It's that heavy. And as soon as you've had one attack your world is rocked because you live in fear of a recurrence. I truly believed that every waking day could be my last. I started to think, *What if they're not panic attacks, and my heart really is about to give out? Or what if a panic attack brings on a heart attack?* The worry was almost enough to bring on an episode. I saw my GP as soon as I got back to Sydney, and filled him in on what had happened. He referred me to an anxiety specialist to help me stay on top of the panic attacks.

But the medication was working and I was able to

prepare for the 2000/01 season. In October 2000 the Australian squad had a pre-season camp at Mooloolaba, on the Sunshine Coast north of Brisbane. Unfortunately, any feelings I had that my world was finally getting back into some kind of order were destroyed when I had another bad turn.

Prior to the camp, I'd played a Pura Cup game in Hobart. (The Pura Cup replaced the Sheffield Shield as Australia's first-class domestic competition in 1999/2000.) We'd had a big night on the turps after the match and I hadn't slept much before taking an early flight to Brisbane. Alcohol doesn't combine too well with antidepressants so I was vulnerable and on edge all day. On the first night in Mooloolaba we gathered for a meeting which was to be addressed by Wayne Bennett, the very successful coach of the Brisbane Broncos rugby league team.

Our new coach, John Buchanan, had just introduced Bennett and he was about to start speaking when I started to hyperventilate. I couldn't catch my breath and had to rush out of the room. As I moved to leave, Allan Border, who was now a selector, grabbed me by the wrist and looked at me as if what I was doing was out of line. But when he saw that my face had gone white and that I was in real trouble, he quickly helped to get me outside. Our physio, Errol Alcott, came out and arranged for me to be taken to hospital. There happened to be a camera crew outside the hotel, who grabbed some footage of me being wheeled into the ambulance. Any chance of hiding the facts about my health problems was gone: the news was well and truly public now.

Fear

I hadn't told anyone in the team about my panic attacks or my use of antidepressants because I'd been feeling on top of the problem since getting back from the UK a few weeks before. I really thought that no one else needed to know. Now all that was changed. The one group of people I didn't want to know (the one group who didn't *need* to know) about my panic attacks had just seen me end up in hospital. When I got there, the doctors asked if I was on any medication. I told them about the antidepressants. Errol heard this and I knew that the team, the ACB and the selectors would know soon enough.

The reality was that I'd let myself down by having a big night in Hobart. Now questions were bound to be asked. The next day I had a meeting with Errol Alcott, Dr Trevor James (the ACB's medico) and the team manager, Steve Bernard. I explained my situation. I told them how and why I'd been prescribed the medication in England. They listened and didn't say much. The next day at the camp I was drug-tested. Testing is supposed to be random, but it didn't seem that way to me. This episode, I feel, was the beginning of the vicious rumours that I was on hard drugs.

A lot of people have panic attacks, but most don't know about them and don't understand them. I'd worked hard to get them under control, but this attack in Mooloolaba blew that right out of the water. My problem was now very public. I think this was the moment that my standing within the cricket world began to suffer. I started to feel quite isolated and there was a lot of talk behind my back. I still don't understand why Cricket Australia (formerly the ACB) didn't take a more positive approach towards me by attempting to understand and fully support one of its contracted players.

Even so, I feel that I battled on quite well. I had a good series against the West Indies that summer, averaging over 50, and made the most runs for either side, a total of 373. I was Man of the Match in the last Test, at the SCG at the start of January, scoring 96 and 86 not out. I really felt that I was on top of everything and my game was firing at a consistently good level. I never lost focus on my cricket.

Despite the odd recurring feelings of anxiety, the anti-depressants I'd been prescribed in England seemed to be working well, bringing my stress levels down to just about normal. Although the truth is that there were probably only a couple of brief periods during my entire career when I felt quite relaxed and secure in the Test team, anxiety just seemed to be part of my makeup. For most of the time in the Australian side I was thinking that I had to work harder to keep my spot, to make sure nothing and nobody could take it away from me. The cliché that says 'You're only as good as your last innings' carries a deep resonance for a cricketer. This is especially so in Australia where there is such a depth of talent that the selectors don't need to persist too long with a player who is not up to scratch.

In my era, there have been many batsmen who've played plenty of Tests for England with batting averages in the mid 30s, but in Australia these players wouldn't have lasted nearly as long. This was a big difference between the two traditional rivals: if you were dropped from the English side there was a good chance you could regain your spot with a few good scores in county cricket; if you were dropped from the Australian team in the 1990s, you faced a tough challenge to return to the side, and we all felt that in our bones.

In spite of my good series against the West Indies in 2000/01, the panic attacks had been a shock to my system. They forced me to reassess what I was doing with my life and sort out what was most valuable to me. I was still living each day feeling it could be my last. It was such an awful feeling – overpowering and frightening. That summer my attacks did begin to ease a little (I only had a few minor ones), but the feeling of dread was still there in the background. And living so much in the public eye made the problem just that bit more difficult to manage.

I knew I had to make some changes in my life. I needed to understand why I was so stressed. Gradually I started to identify the things that might've been contributing to the anxiety and I realised that my marriage was no longer happy for me. I'd let it drift along for far too long and my non-stop cricket lifestyle was only making that situation worse.

The seeds of doubt about the wisdom of getting married that I'd felt way back on the 1993 Ashes tour had begun to bear some very heavy fruit. But I had no idea that the tension that existed between Steph and me was about to explode – nor that my career and life were about to go into a tailspin.

Drinks Break
Tugga

For much of his career Steve Waugh was known as 'the Iceman'. To us of course, and legions of cricket fans, he was 'Tugga', but this other nickname came from the media and his opponents, because that was how they perceived him. Tugga and I had an uneasy relationship. It was a strange one — there seemed to be a tension between us, hovering just below the surface. I think it really came down to a difference in personalities, but at times those differences did boil over into outright confrontation.

I first met Steve when I was working for Bob Radford at the NSWCA in York Street. Apart from my main responsibility as head barman for Bob — not a bad gig, all things considered — I also looked after the state squad's clothing. If a player needed a new cap or jumper or any other gear early in the season, I was the go-to guy. One afternoon, I remember bringing in some new travel pants for the guys to try on, and Steve made it well known that he thought they sucked. There were always some guys who liked them and some who didn't, and it was quite clear that Tugga was firmly in the latter camp.

Not too long after that, I first made the state squad, but I always felt a bit nervous when he was around — his manner just seemed to unsettle me. To me, he was rather unemotional and had little personal warmth. I didn't think he was much of a communicator. Although, as I learned later, he gave advice and encouragement in his own unique way and probably wasn't aware of how he could be perceived by others.

Down the track I did realise that I wasn't the only person who felt uncomfortable in his presence, but because I was so sensitive it's possible I let his manner affect me more than others did. Steve's eyes could send a chill through you, and he never said a lot, even at the best of times. I'm not sure whether he was trying to sort the mentally weak from the strong, the genuine from the false – or whether he just enjoyed mind games – but he certainly put me on edge right from the get-go.

For eight years Steve and I were in the same Australian team, sharing hotels and dressing rooms all over the cricket world. It took a while, but eventually I started getting used to his manner, his dry sense of humour and his steeliness. In many ways, he was the same man off the field as he was in the centre. But he could also be very funny in a dry, slightly sardonic way, and when he kicked back he was a lot of fun.

There were loads of times when Steve and I were the first guys in the team to launch into the Cold Chisel classic 'Khe Sanh' during victory celebrations. He was often the instigator of team get-togethers and was a great tourist, someone who always had his camera ready and was keen to get out of the comfort zone of the hotel and soak up the local culture. In the early 1990s he began writing his diaries and recording his travels, and he's done very well with these books. Early in my career I also enjoyed getting out of the hotel and exploring places, particularly when we were on the subcontinent. Whether it was down to the Ganges in India, the bazaars in Pakistan or the coastline in Sri

Lanka, just like Steve, I also found these places fascinating, so different from what we were used to back home. And the people, all cricket-lovers of course, made us feel very welcome.

Tugga would usually be the first one to organise a day trip or excursion. There were times during these trips when I definitely thought I'd worked him out – that I'd 'got' him. And we usually did get on well, away from the paddock. Despite our clashes, I think we both had immense respect for each other. I am pretty sure he respected the way I played, and at times he made some really generous statements about my game. Even in 2001 shortly after I was dropped, he said that my first innings of the First Test really set the mood for us throughout the entire Ashes series. He has also said that I had the quickest feet in the game, and the best technique of all the batsmen in world cricket when in form. It always came as a surprise when he made such big statements. He didn't do it that often so it really hit home when he did, and I took these rare outbursts as great compliments.

Nevertheless, there was a tendency for Steve and me to get on each other's nerves. I think it was just a case of two very different people spending months of the year in each other's pockets. In that kind of situation, even when you're good mates, things can get a little strained. I am sure a lot of people would struggle in such a tight team situation. I was always fairly hyper-active in the dressing room and around the team. I was also too sensitive at times and could have off days when I was worrying about something and was possibly a little difficult to be around. When I was in one of these moods – and most cricketers have them – it was just weird how the one guy who could make me feel uncomfortable was Steve. It was especially tricky when he was the captain of the team, the guy whom you'd hope to consult if you had any hassles.

Despite our difficulty at times communicating on a personal level, Steve was an amazing leader and captain. His dogged determination and killer instinct were unmatched. He was definitely the man you wanted next to you when things got tough – I think difficult situations brought out the best in him. He led by example and spoke with both his bat and his body language, which were always an inspiration to me. His four at the SCG in January 2003 to bring up that century on the last ball of the day's play against England was the ultimate example of his inspirational character as a cricketer. When the selectors were nervous about his future and the media had written him off, he came out and proved them all wrong. He had amazing determination and focus.

There's no doubt that Steve Waugh is a legend of the game, loved and respected by all. The problems he and I encountered were at times my fault, at other times Steve's. Even though I've now retired, I still feel a little uneasy about how Steve handled some situations involving me, particularly my final dropping in August 2001. But I also feel greatly honoured and privileged to have played all but a few of my 74 Test matches with a player of his quality. We all continue to grow up and move on, and I'm hoping that one day, not too far away, Tugga and I can sit down over a beer and chew the fat about our cricketing days together.

Chapter 10

Wild is the Wind

2001

Stephanie and I broke up two weeks before the tour to India in early 2001. It was without doubt the toughest decision I've had to make in my life and it certainly wasn't taken lightly. At the time I felt the need to be honest and open with my feelings rather than hold them back as I'd done for so long. Initially, the plan was to have a temporary break so I could work through my inner turmoil. I didn't want to become another divorce statistic, but I knew that happiness was important in life, and I just wasn't finding that in our marriage. In particular, the subject of children was the catalyst for our break-up. Steph wanted children but I just couldn't commit to the idea because I wasn't happy. And yet I also understood Steph's position. I realised that after seven-and-a-half years it was natural to be thinking about kids. But I couldn't see it. I just didn't feel ready.

I finally found the courage to drop this bombshell one afternoon while sitting around the edge of our pool in Queens Park. Although I'm sure Steph must have sensed that certain things weren't great, to say that she was totally shocked and upset would be an understatement. We decided that because I was leaving for India within two weeks, Steph would stay with some close friends until I went on tour and then move back to our place.

Just before the Indian tour, the annual Allan Border Medal ceremony was held in Melbourne. It's a huge night on the cricket calendar, probably the biggest event of the year, and it's telecast live around the country. Because of our recent split, I was going to the dinner solo.

The news of our break-up had gone round the team pretty quickly, relaying from the players to their wives and partners. They'd all be there at the Border Medal night and I knew that my behaviour was going to be closely watched. I was very nervous because I thought the general opinion would be that it was all my fault and I feared everyone's eyes would be burning holes in the back of my head. I knew the wives and girlfriends would rally around Steph. They were a close-knit group whose lives were often extremely difficult, with their husbands, fiancés or boy-friends away so much and their relationships depending largely on trust.

It was a very fractured existence, we lived our lives together in segments. It was always harder for our partners, because we were the ones off on another trip, another adventure, going after our dreams, while they were often stuck at home, without their other half.

Although the girls hadn't seen Stephanie since the split, some of them had called her to offer their support and disbelief at what was happening. Rightly or wrongly, they'd think I was the bad guy. That was just the natural order of things.

To survive this big night in the best way possible, I had decided that I'd take it easy on the grog. I knew the only chance of something untoward happening was if I were drinking and getting a little too loose. My decision to drink in moderation ran against my instincts, because I'd usually see the Allan Border Medal night as a way of celebrating another big Australian cricketing season, so I'd relax, have a few grogs and enjoy myself, like most of the other guys. But this year the plan was to stay cool, be low-key, have a couple of glasses of wine and get through it.

But it didn't quite turn out that way. Typically, as at most functions, the waiters hover eagerly around you, topping up your glass. Sometimes you don't even notice your glass has had another refill. It's their job, but at the end of the function you have no idea how much you've drunk, other than how sloshed you feel.

A few days before, we'd been told that Jimmy Barnes was going to perform. And because Cold Chisel's 'Khe Sanh' was one of the first songs we'd crank up in the dressing room after winning a Test match, Channel 9 had asked five of us to get up and sing along with the iron-throated Barnesy. But on the day, the TV guys became nervous, thinking the singalong might detract from having Jimmy Barnes there – and perhaps some of the players might not even know the words. Maybe Jimmy himself baulked at the idea, who knows? Instead, Channel 9 decided that Jimmy would walk through the audience and get some of us to shout a few lyrics into his mic.

Jimmy closed the night. By this time I must have polished off a bottle and half of red wine and was feeling pretty charged and *very* relaxed. I was sitting next to my old friends Adam and Mel Gilchrist, and we were very merry at this stage. Thankfully, Steph's name hadn't really come up in conversation. But now, with several drinks on board, the question was eventually posed by Gilly and Mel: 'What's going on?' I gave only a brief explanation. It was far too raw and painful to discuss in depth and I was still very confused about it all.

As Jimmy started belting out that Aussie rock anthem in his unmistakable raspy voice, I waited eagerly for him to come down to our table. But he didn't. Instead he stayed on stage, singing the song as a duet with his son, David Campbell. Gilly and Mel started egging me on, saying, 'Come on, Slats. Aren't you going to get up there?' The alcohol had relaxed me and after the third or fourth nudge from them, I figured, *Why not?* It wasn't as if it would be the first time I'd done something like that. I was well known as the guy who loved to jump up on a table and dance or sing, or get up on stage with a band in a pub and give it my all. I always took my guitar on tour with me and loved to get into music. I'm into all kinds of singers and bands, from Bon Jovi to Green Day, Pete Murray to Silverchair, and lots more. My record collection is truly all over the musical shop.

So as far as I was concerned, it was nothing out of the

ordinary when I finally got up on stage to help Jimmy and David belt out the song. My team-mates had seen it all before. The guys who knew me just thought, *Well, that's Slats*, and went back to having a good time. I still laugh about it, in fact, although I think the mistake I made was in taking a glass of red wine up on stage with me. I still reckon I didn't spill a drop (quite skilful, really), but I know it didn't look too flash.

I'll never forget coming off the stage after singing with Jimmy (I'm not sure if he loved or hated what I did) and how as I passed Denis Rogers, the ACB chairman at the time, he leapt out of his seat and gave me a huge bear hug. 'That's the best thing I've ever seen,' he told me. 'Well done!' Just for a moment, I'd thought he was going to reprimand me, so that was a relief.

Naively, I figured there'd been no harm done. My team-mates couldn't believe I'd got up there. They were all laughing, saying 'You're mad' or 'Well done, I loved it.' I actually didn't see the footage until early in 2005 when I appeared on the Andrew Denton show *Enough Rope*. I have to admit, I was totally shocked at how drunk and messy I looked. It wasn't one of my best performances, that's for sure!

The backlash came later. A groundswell of bad feeling towards me had been building for some time, and my impromptu stage performance became part of a series of things I'd done that were considered to have gone beyond the limits of rationality. However, at the time it had seemed innocuous, a bit of fun for everybody. I was willing to get up and have a go. I wondered what was wrong with that.

It was a tough period for me. I felt as if I were in a different world from everyone else. My life had changed completely because of a decision I'd made to put my marriage on hold so I could work through my troubles – and I had great hopes for reconciliation, at least initially. I'm sure most people who go through this feel as if everything in their lives has changed. The people around me probably thought it was a rash decision on my part, a typically impulsive act, because they hadn't seen it coming. But things hadn't been going well in my personal life for quite some time.

I'd been fighting an ongoing battle with myself, too, because my parents had split up when I was twelve and I was determined never to do the same. I saw marriage as sacred; and if there were troubles, you tried to work them through. That was part of marriage. But I also felt that things weren't right with Steph and me. It's no doubt true that I got so close to Stephanie and married her when we were fairly young because of what had happened with my mother.

Going through my teenage years without my mother, I'm sure I drew strength and security from my relationship with Stephanie. Her family was very warm and loving, and as I've said, I spent a lot of time at the Blackett household in Wagga. I soaked up the loving closeness of their family which I felt I lacked. Steph filled a void in my life. She's a wonderful person and she was incredibly supportive throughout my early career. There was no doubting my love for her.

It does seem that in my teens I was looking for a stable relationship with a woman to replace the one with my mother, which had ended so abruptly. I've read a lot about this sort of thing since and I'm convinced that the strongest relationship for any young boy growing into manhood is with his mother. That's the first true relationship you have with a woman, so you have an expectation of women based on your own mother–son relationship. Stephanie was my childhood sweetheart and we were married when we were both just 23. Looking back now, I can't believe we married so young. I mean, you know so little about yourself and life at that age. What made our situation harder was that my dream of playing cricket for Australia had just become a reality and my life suddenly changed dramatically.

In my family we married young, and I had no example of an alternative. My older brother Julian, whom I idolised, had married his childhood sweetheart at the age of 22. My sister Tracey married her first serious boyfriend when she was in her early twenties. Because of this, I thought it was okay to get married young. I think it would've been very different for me, and for Stephanie, if I'd had an older brother and sister who believed that your early twenties were a time for exploring life and learning about yourself, not getting married.

However, marriage was also a stabilising force for me as I worked my way through local cricket and out into the larger world of professional sport. It gave me the love and support that helped me wash away a lot of the insecurities I'm sure would have plagued me if I wasn't in a close relationship. Having been selected in the NSW team fairly quickly, I'd had a good first season and raced into the Australian team as an engaged man – all too suddenly I was living out my dream. I was on an Ashes tour and the world just opened up for me. It was like I'd been struck by a bolt of lightning.

It had started perfectly: I'd scored that big hundred in my second Test match, at Lord's of all places. I was seeing a totally different world and towards the end of the 1993 tour I was starting to question whether getting married was really the right thing to do at that stage in my life. But I knew deep down I didn't have the strength to change anything. The temptations I faced on the Ashes tour created a state of confusion and at the time I wasn't sure if it was normal to feel like that. I now realise it was absolutely natural given my circumstances, and I've noticed that every one of my former team-mates has gone through the same thing at times. It was just part of being in an elite group of cricketers travelling the world together. It took amazing strength and willpower to avoid giving into temptation.

As I've said, Stephanie came over for about two weeks right in the middle of that 1993 tour, and we had a difficult trot. When she saw that my time was taken up with the game and everything that went with it, she felt insecure. But it was hard for me to settle her insecurities because the lifestyle was new to me, too. I didn't quite understand it myself. Steph didn't know what to expect now that I was in the Australian team, which was a full-on commitment and I wanted to go for it totally. Steph could see that the life we'd lived since school had changed – and she was no longer the centre of my attention.

The day before Steph left to go home in June 1993 we'd actually thought about putting off the wedding again. I still believed that Stephanie was the girl for me but I wondered whether we were rushing things. We were both having second thoughts and wondered if we should wait a couple of years to see how we'd cope with such a different lifestyle. Looking back, I can see that I was greener than most young players who make the Test side, mainly because the AS had kept me at home a lot when I first moved to Sydney, a time when otherwise I'd have been getting out and learning more about life.

It's said in top-level cricket that there's a system and it gets everyone eventually. By the system, people mean the lifestyle – the opportunities that open up, the temptations to do things you wouldn't normally do, especially with the women who make themselves available to cricketers and other sportsmen. I'd heard about this but said to myself, *No, it's not going to get me. I'm strong, I know where I'm at.*

But the temptations I'd had as a state player were minor compared to those that appeared once I started travelling around England as a member of the Australian cricket team. Suddenly you're famous. You're mixing with rock stars and actors, and other celebrities who tell you that all they ever wanted to be was a famous cricketer. It's a real test of your character. You're tempted all the way and it takes a very strong person to rise above it. These were some of the reasons I'd been worried about getting married. And even though I settled back into some kind of normality after that 1993 tour, I do think the pressures of international cricket led to my split from Stephanie early in 2001.

The day after the Allan Border Medal and my drunken duet with Barnesy, I headed off to India with the Australian team. There was a lot of pre-tour hype predicting that the 2001 Border-Gavaskar Trophy was going to be a huge series, which it turned out to be. Some say it was the greatest three-Test series of all time. It would certainly be hard to beat for the drama, the tightness of the results, the turnaround by the home side and the spectacular quality of the play.

Leading up to India 2001, we'd won fifteen Tests on the trot, which was a new world record. I was one of only four guys to have played in every one of those matches (Justin Langer, Mark Waugh and NSW pace bowler Glenn McGrath were the other three). We were on a roll and it seemed that we had our best chance to beat India at home for the first time since Bill Lawry's team won a series there in 1969/70. Because of our momentum and form leading up to this tour, the mood in the camp was buoyant and we believed we could finally nail the Indians on the dusty, spinning wickets in their own backyard.

But before we'd left for India, on the day before the Border Medal — when we were in Melbourne doing publicity, collecting our touring gear and being briefed by the ACB — the biggest bombshell of my career was dropped on me. When I checked into my hotel room, I received a phone call from the team manager, Steve Bernard. The Australian Cricket Board's CEO, Malcolm Speed, had asked Steve to find out if I had a drug problem. I was stunned. Straightaway, I told him the truth.

'I certainly don't have a drug problem, Steve,' I said. 'And please understand that this is a huge allegation. I would like you to tell Malcolm that he should've come to see me in person about this.'

Having nearly fallen over in shock, I was furious about what had just occurred – and I couldn't believe that such an accusation had been made by phone. It was a joke.

That afternoon we had a number of meetings, the last of which was a briefing from Malcolm Speed regarding the upcoming tour. At the conclusion he pulled me aside and said he wanted to clear something up. I knew what was coming. He said he'd learned from a very reliable source that I had a drug problem, a *serious* drug problem.

'What do you mean, "serious"?' I asked.

'Cocaine, heroin ... that sort of thing,' he replied.

I was flabbergasted. I couldn't believe what I was hearing and became as angry with him as I had earlier with Bernard. I was quite literally shaking with rage.

'You are kidding, Malcolm,' I said. 'That's *completely ridiculous*. Apart from a couple of puffs on a joint a year ago, as most people do at some stage, drugs have never been a part of my life. Never *will* be a part of my life. I'm not saying I'm a saint, but drugs will never enter my life. You tell your source he's not as reliable as he thinks.' This was completely true, of course, as I couldn't even handle marijuana, which is widely regarded as a weak drug.

'And you get ASDA to come and drug-test me now,' I continued, referring to the Australian Sports Drug Agency. 'And tell them they can test me every day for as long as they – or you – want! They won't find anything. I want you to do that because I don't think you understand what a heavy accusation you've made.'

I'd had great respect for what Malcolm Speed was doing for Australian cricket up to this moment. But in that instant, it was lost. How could a man in his position handle this situation so badly?

Speed then backed off and said he believed me. He told me to forget all about it and have a great tour of India, as if it were just a simple misunderstanding. I was never able to find out who Speed's 'source' was, but my instincts told me there was a strong chance it was someone in-house, so to speak. I really hope I'm wrong.

It took a while for the pieces to fall into place, but I finally worked out a possible reason for these rumours. In the lead-up to our Indian tour, Steve Waugh had gone around to have a private chat with Steph after we'd split up. Steve had replaced Tubby as captain of the Australian side in February 1999. As soon as he left, Stephanie rang me to say that Steve had just landed on her doorstep and that they'd talked for quite a while – which was a total surprise to me. He told Steph he thought that I needed assistance. He said he'd found a doctor in Double Bay who could 'help' me. Steph said Tugga seemed concerned, and she mentioned the name of this fellow Steve thought I should go and see.

I wanted to do the right thing by the team and, given that my captain had recommended this doctor, I did go to see him. It was a bizarre experience. He was a doctor who'd moved away from traditional medicine into more alternative treatments. On that first visit he slapped me with a vitamin B injection in my backside, put me on a vitamin C drip and then talked to me about my immune system.

He also talked about my anxiety and the panic attacks, but made no mention of drugs. He said he dealt with cases like mine all the time and that the solution was to boost my immune system. He made out that he didn't know much about me, but I think he had been given a brief by someone – possibly Steve, possibly someone else – though I'm not sure. I was a little concerned though when I found out that I couldn't claim for the visit or any medicines through my health fund.

The doctor ended up convincing me that I should buy enough vitamin shots for the Indian tour and administer them myself, which was a pretty scary thought. It ended up costing me a small fortune. I walked out of his office with a brown paper bag full of vials of vitamins B and C and another bag full of syringes. I can only think that the subsequent accusations about heroin and me arose because the syringes had been spotted when my baggage was x-rayed on the way from Sydney to Melbourne. Either that, or someone in-house had some concerns of their own.

But surely Malcolm, and anyone else who seriously thought that I might have been using heroin, had some idea of what it does to people. Did they really think I could've maintained a solid career as an international cricketer, a professional athlete, and been using narcotics? Where were the needle marks on my arms or body? How could I possibly function in the day-to-day routine of travel, practice and play, and be a junkie at the same time? Did I have suppliers all over the cricket world to keep me going? It was completely ridiculous and showed how naive some people were. And I had been drug-tested several times during the year and my career. All of these had come back negative. Which of course made perfect sense — because I didn't use drugs.

Admittedly, the incident in England in 2000 with the joint of marijuana might have fuelled rumours. Yet surely anyone with a clue knows that there is a huge difference between a few silly puffs on a joint and a heroin habit. This was another in a series of absurd rumours that were to plague me for the next two years. Shane Warne has often said his life sometimes resembles a soap opera. I was soon to realise that mine did too, even if it wasn't quite so public. But because I was on the receiving end of rumours and innuendo, rather than well-publicised troubles like Warnie's, my difficulties were harder for me to control because I was never quite sure exactly what was being whispered about me. And all this came before the biggest tour of our careers.

● ⑩ ●

In many ways it was a relief to get to India that February, even if it was obvious that we had an incredibly tough and challenging tour ahead. At least I felt that I could get away from some of the negative things that had been happening. I could lose myself in the cocoon-like life of a cricketing tour and concentrate on my game.

I decided that it would be best to clear the air with the team before the tour started, so I rang Steve Waugh's room soon after we arrived, and asked him to come up for a chat. I told him that at the end of our next team meeting I wanted to have a few words to the squad regarding my marriage split. I preferred to get things out in the open, rather than have people wondering what was going on or talking about it behind my back. Steve thought that was a good idea.

But at the meeting, as soon as I began to talk to the rest of the team, I started to feel uneasy. It wasn't coming out right and I knew it had been a mistake. Suddenly it felt as if I were making excuses, or somehow trying to justify myself, when I really didn't need to. But still I went through with it, talking about my marriage split, trying to reassure everyone that I was fine and totally focused on the tour. No one said much afterwards, which made me feel awful. Perhaps it would have been better to carry on as if nothing had happened, rather than responding to the rumours about what I was going through.

I started the tour pretty flat. I didn't get runs in the opening games and didn't feel that I was playing well. This was not surprising, given what had been happening off the field. Still, I carried on as best I could. But then I was hit with my next haymaker. Just before the First Test in Mumbai, during the final warm-up match, Steve 'Brute' Bernard pulled me aside for another chat. We were batting and I was already out for a low score. We relocated to the far end of the open-air viewing room.

He started by telling me it was a bit awkward for him, but that he needed to clear something up and was acting on orders from Malcolm Speed. He then handed me a printout of an email the ACB had received alleging I was the father of a child in Tasmania. Once again, I was dumb-struck.

'That's ridiculous,' I said. 'It's impossible. Physically impossible! And you tell Malcolm Speed if he wants to find out about this he can come over here and ask me face to face. Or, at worst, he can ring me and not get you to do it again!'

I then looked closely at the email.

'Brute,' I said, 'do you realise this was sent at 3.40 on a Saturday morning and the sender's name is that of a man? Don't you think that looks a bit suspicious? Doesn't it look like he was just playing a prank? Maybe he was with his mates, all of them pissed out of their heads ...'

My tone was controlled but firm. Brute was only the messenger and quickly realised that he should have looked more closely at the email before waving it around in front of me. It was obviously a wind-up from some pissed idiot. My life had started to become public and this bloke obviously wanted to jump on the bandwagon.

Not only was this accusation ridiculous, but just like the drugs rumour, it gave me the impression – understandably, I think – that no one trusted me. The people with whom I dealt closely in my professional life seemed very suspicious of me. They were prepared to believe the worst and swallow whatever rumours happened to be out there. And there always seemed to be plenty of them.

From that unpleasant moment on, I had to try to put my head down and get some runs, despite all the negative forces at work around me. But I'd never been the kind of guy to lock myself away in my room on tour and think about cricket every minute. I'd gone stir crazy on a few occasions through spending too much time alone, particularly during a match. It allowed for far too much thinking space.

I'd always found the best way for me to cope with the pressures and lifestyle was to make sure I went out at night to a restaurant with a few team-mates. And despite all the accusations and conflicts, my behaviour was fine early in the tour, I thought, apart from my lack of runs in the games leading up to the First Test. But I was hearing terrible whispers about my getting up on stage with Jimmy Barnes, that it was out of line at that sort of event (which seems pretty funny to me) and that it showed no respect for Stephanie, given that we had just split up. There's no doubt that I now totally regretted my duet with Barnesy. It was stupid to draw unnecessary attention to myself and, true, it didn't show a lot of support for Stephanie at all. There was no point dwelling on it, though. It was done, I had to get on with things.

So I was in a weird space on that tour, feeling emotionally low and physically weak. I was feeling so odd, in fact, that I'd started smoking. I'd always been very anti-smoking and I'd often preach to smokers about the terrible health consequences. That I'd taken it up myself sums up the state I was in at the time. Warnie and Colin Miller were regular smokers, and there were a few casual choofers, and now me, the new bad boy. Damien Martyn and I liked to hang out in the hotel and have a few smokes together while chatting about the day's play or whatever else was on our minds. I got on well with 'Marto', and I'm sure that if my behaviour had gone over the line, he would have said something to me.

And then, with all the hype building madly, not just in Mumbai but across the whole of India, I was involved in another drama. A few days prior to the Test, after the tour match in Mumbai where I'd had my talk with Bernard, I had a few drinks one night with some team-mates. This is quite a common occurrence, particularly during a tour match – and during the 1970s and '80s it would have happened every night. Anyway, I went out with a few team-mates and it ended up being a pretty big night for everyone. At a team meeting soon afterwards, coach John Buchanan decided to play bad cop. This was totally out of character for the guy. I was the first person he singled out at the team meeting.

'Slats,' he said to me, but indirectly to the entire team, 'give yourself a chance. How are you going to perform by staying out late and drinking the amount you're drinking?'

I sat back in my chair, stunned. I hadn't had many late nights, apart from the one just mentioned, and that was before a day off. I knew myself and how much I could handle. And I was hardly the Lone Ranger – every time I'd been out, I'd been with fellow players.

The way I saw it, Buchanan was relaying a directive he'd received from someone else (I don't know who), because it wasn't like the coach to make that sort of announcement. I didn't come back at him at the meeting. Normally I would have if I thought it was a false accusation, but this time I felt there was no point. There were things happening here that I simply couldn't control. It was almost as if I were becoming resigned to the existence of these crazy rumours and innuendoes about me, so I just sat there. Then

Buchanan gave Mark Waugh a going over about his contribution to the team. It just wasn't the right forum in which to raise these issues.

At that meeting in Mumbai, Buchanan totally lost me, and 'Junior' was pretty pissed off too. To his eternal credit, Matthew Hayden put his hand up and supported both of us. He said the comments weren't accurate. You could tell from the look on Buchanan's face that he knew he'd made a big blunder. We wound up the meeting and I went straight back to my room, where my Marlboro Lights were fast becoming my new best friend. About an hour later there was a knock at the door. It was Buchanan. Even now, several years later, I still can't believe his first line.

'Oh, you're not going to like me again, are you?' he said.

He then apologised profusely and admitted that taking me to task in a team meeting had been the wrong thing to do.

I wasn't going to let him off this lightly. 'You're damn right it was the wrong thing to do,' I replied. 'You've always portrayed yourself as a rounded person, a family man, someone who wants happy cricketers off the field.'

I went on to say that I wasn't having a happy time because I was going through some personal difficulties and I thought he'd understand that. I also said that if he thought there was a problem with me, he should come to me in private and discuss it. I told him that I knew he was only relaying someone else's opinion, doing their spade work for them.

'Why didn't you come and knock on my door *before* the

meeting?' I asked. 'You've now made a very difficult situation for me.'

Buchanan apologised again and said he hoped we could move on. This seemed to me an unusual response. I was grateful for an apology, but his admission that he'd done the wrong thing so soon after the event was strange, given that only an hour earlier he'd tried to play the tough guy in front of the team – which really wasn't his style.

So all this had happened – the Border Medal night, Malcolm Speed accusing me of using drugs, an accusation I'd fathered a child in Tasmania, and now a jibe from the team coach, in front of the other players, that I was drinking too much – and we hadn't even played the First Test. At least with the match about to start, I thought I could now concentrate on what was really important. That's what I was in India for. But there was to be one more incident, this time of my own doing, that dragged things down even further for me.

On the second day of the First Test, which ran from 27 February to 1 March 2001 in Mumbai, we were heading towards a great win when Rahul Dravid pulled a ball from Damien Fleming to me at square leg. I expected the ball to reach me comfortably, but at times it's hard to judge catches when fielding square of the wicket. Suddenly I was forced to dive forward and I took a good low catch. Or at least *I* was sure, 100 per cent sure, that I'd caught it. Dravid stood his ground, understandably, and umpire Srinivas Venkataraghavan (known as Venkat) then referred the decision to the third umpire.

After I'd come up with the ball and seen Dravid

standing his ground, I said to the batsman: 'I caught that. I caught that.' He shrugged as if to say he wanted the umpires to decide. So I went over to Venkat and told him I'd caught it. I wished he'd have simply asked me if I had taken the catch. But he didn't.

Instead he said: 'Well, what do I do? I couldn't see it. The square-leg umpire couldn't see it because you were in front of him. Dravid hasn't walked, so *he's* not sure. So this is what I'm meant to do: go to the third umpire.'

Then I looked at Dravid and said: 'Mate, I'm not a cheat. I wouldn't cheat you out. I'm 100 per cent sure I caught it.'

'Well, what am *I* supposed to do?' Dravid said. 'You guys do it [stand your ground and wait for the umpire's decision]. I didn't see it carry, so I'm waiting for the decision.'

Again, I told him that I wasn't a cheat and that he should've walked. As I walked away, he said: 'Fuck you. Fuck you.' I then turned around and came back at him. That's when things started to look pretty ugly. I insisted that I wasn't a cheat – but I was angry, and the oft-repeated footage from our clash shows that.

I don't blame Dravid. If he didn't see me take the catch clearly he was within his rights to stay there and leave it to the umpires. I was never a walker myself. I believed that you got four maybe five rough decisions in a season, so if you could pick up one or two the umpire misses, then good on you. But by not walking, Dravid seemed to me to be indicating that he wasn't prepared to take my word for it. In the state of mind I was in at the time, Dravid became just one more person who didn't trust me. The bubble that had been building in me over the previous few months was now expanding rapidly, and – unfortunately – it just so happened to burst on the field that day. Feeling that my honesty as a cricketer had been questioned was all it took for me to blow a valve.

Perhaps Steve Waugh could've taken me in hand, but it's hard for a captain when a player is going off – and I was seeing red. Even if Steve had told me to calm down, I would've said what I said regardless. Matty Hayden supported me by having a go at Dravid, although neither he nor anyone else told me to cool it. But heated moments on the field are hard to judge and sometimes a reaction from the captain in such situations makes it looks worse. West Indian skipper Richie Richardson had tried to calm Curtly Ambrose when he and Steve Waugh were going at it in Trinidad a few years earlier, but Richardson's intervention actually made their clash look worse. (The picture of him trying to pull Ambrose away looked pretty bad.)

In retrospect, it was no great surprise that Dravid wasn't given out. In a close call, the video replays are often not good enough for a clear decision to be made and so the batsman gets the benefit of the doubt. But I say I caught it cleanly and I'll say that until the day I die. The ball wedged into my hand, which was on the grass. I kept the ball off the ground. What I said to batsman and umpire wasn't bad – I just kept repeating, 'I'm not a cheat, and I wouldn't claim the catch if I wasn't 100 per cent sure I'd caught it' – but my gestures did look bad, worse than they really were.

When we came off for lunch soon after the incident, the match referee, Cammie Smith, came down to tell me that although it didn't look good, the umpires hadn't reported me. Venkat had told him the clash hadn't been that serious. It was a very regrettable incident and I wish I'd been able to vent my frustrations in another way, but that's how I seem to operate – I lock things up and then bang, everything comes out at once. It hadn't helped that we'd had a minute of silence before the game to mark the death of cricketing legend Sir Donald Bradman. To me, that made my reaction to the Dravid catch seem even less dignified.

Today, having worked on TV, I can see that incidents like that one in Mumbai are replayed to death, which makes them appear increasingly worse. I did look very angry, but my words were not as bad as my body language, although these days you'd be reported just because it looked bad. Such scrutiny has tightened up considerably. In my case Cammie Smith was probably fairly lenient, but he was guided by Venkat.

After play ended that day I found Rahul Dravid and explained the catch from my point of view, and apologised for having lost my temper. We had a brief chat outside the Indian dressing room and Dravid was fine about it. I saw him the next day and have seen a lot of him since – especially as I now do some commentary in India – and I've never sensed a problem between us. I've even referred to it in my commentary a few times. During the Australian tour to India in 2004, Dravid got a bit heated during a tense moment in the Fourth Test, again in Mumbai, so I made a comment on ABC Radio that there must be something about this ground that produces bad behaviour.

If I'd sworn at the umpire and really carved him up

verbally, I would've been on report instantly. But on the day I wasn't reported, not by Venkat nor by Smith. I had a clean record before that match and it didn't look as if the incident would cause any further problems. Two days later, however, I *was* reported. In the lead-up to the Second Test I made a comment to radio station 2WS back home. I was their cricket reporter and I'd speak to them on most days of a Test match. They wanted a statement from me about my outburst the day before, so in no more than two sentences I tried to make sense of it. I said something along the lines of: 'I feel sure I took the catch cleanly and I didn't understand the need for the third umpire to get involved. I reacted badly to the not-out verdict, but it looked so much worse than it actually was. There's been a big overreaction.'

While apparently harmless, my comment somehow breached ICC regulations. Steve Bernard told me in Kolkata, prior to the Second Test, which began on 11 March, that I'd been reported for the radio interview. I couldn't believe it. At the hearing, Venkat said that in hindsight he probably should've reported me during the match. My penalty was a one-match suspension. I was amazed by this but I kept my cool. I told Cammie Smith that I hoped he understood what this meant for an Australian cricketer: not only would it make me the first player from any country to be suspended from a Test match, but it could imperil my position in the team, given the competitive environment of the Australian team and our depth of cricket talent. Smith understood, but felt that a one-match suspension was fair, if harsh. I disagreed.

Since I hadn't been reported for the actual incident, how on earth could I be reported and suspended for a brief radio interview?

Steve Waugh backed me strongly during the hearing, to his credit. He and team manager Steve Bernard gave me a look to let me know that they would take over the argument. Waugh then explained how tough it might be for me to get back into the Australian team, adding that with criticism from the press this might even end my career. Tugga was fantastic in this meeting and Bernard backed him up very strongly. Eventually Smith changed the punishment to a fine of half my match fee (which came to about $3500) and a six-month suspended ban for one Test match. It was a big win for me, and an instance when Steve Waugh truly defended me.

The Dravid incident was my response to all the things going on around me leading into that Test. When I decided to split from Stephanie I immediately wondered whether I'd done the right thing. I'm sure most people in that situation go through that – I'd like to think my mother did. Suddenly for the first time in my adult life I wasn't in a relationship and it was scary, weird and liberating all at once. Deep down I thought it was the right thing to do, however hard it was to get through. But then the accusations and character judgments began hitting me during the first weeks of the tour. It seemed my every move was being questioned off the field and now the Dravid incident made me feel I was being questioned on the field as well. That was hard.

That 2001 India tour is still talked about as one of the

toughest of all time, and justifiably so. The cricket was incredibly intense and close. I didn't perform too badly, although my scores weren't huge. I didn't make runs in the first innings in Mumbai and I was 19 not out in the second innings when we won on the third day. In the Second Test in Kolkata, which India won in a remarkable comeback, I got two 40s and didn't bat too badly. During the Third Test (in Chennai, on 18–22 March), the decider which India won in a tense finish, I nicked one early off Zaheer Khan in the first innings and then in the second innings, when I really thought I was set, I got 48.

My basic breakdown for any three-match series was to get three starts and convert them, ideally, into two centuries and a half-century. In doing that, you can average 45–50 on a tour and contribute heavily to the team's fortunes. I averaged 30 in that series so it wasn't too bad, given that we lost and several guys struggled more than I did. But every series in India is tough for a batsman. You can get out at any time there: they always have two good spinners and with the slightly uneven bounce of their wickets, you're never as fully set as you would be in Australia or England, or even in Pakistan, where the pitches can be pretty flat. But unfortunately for me, the innuendo swirling around off the field marred that great India tour of 2001.

Chapter 11

Misunderstood

2001

I have often wondered what would have happened on the 2001 Ashes tour, my last series as a Test player, had Mark Taylor still been captain. He was a guy I really trusted, someone who would have given me some tough but helpful advice when I really needed it. Tubby could be very direct but you always knew where you stood with him – and that's essential in the hothouse atmosphere of a Test tour.

My Ashes tour started strangely. The one-day series was scheduled first, through the month of June, which meant that I and a few others who weren't involved in the pyjama game (like Justin Langer and Colin Miller) were set to arrive after the one-day side. Again, because of this scheduling, Channel 4 asked if I wanted to call the one-day series for them. I was keen, and I also thought it would be good to be in England at the start of the northern summer, rather than being stuck at home at the beginning of our winter. At least that way I could have some net sessions, get used to the English conditions again and work my way into the tour gradually. The ACB gave me permission to go, so I was there good and early. It seemed like the perfect preparation.

During commentary downtime, I'd get some bowlers together and we'd have a few good net sessions. By the time Langer and Miller arrived, my game was feeling pretty solid. When I told Justin what I'd been doing, he said that all he'd been able to do in Perth was have a few unsatisfactory indoor nets. He thought it was a smart move on my part to go to England early. At the same time, there was an awkwardness between the one-day and Test squads: because the Test-only players like me were not part of the full tour, my early presence put a few people off. There were whispers about whether I wanted to be a commentator or a player. This came back to haunt me when Steve Waugh was handing down my sentence later in the tour.

I felt that commentating was good for my game and a great way to prepare for the upcoming Ashes series. It was also a terrific career opportunity and one that didn't intrude on my training. I had my net sessions at the grounds – in English light, on local pitches – and watching from the commentary box gave me a different take on the game, a more analytical view that I felt could flow into my play. It was all good.

The distinction between the two squads had already played out during the one-day team's stopover in Gallipoli, the first time an Australian team had visited the site of the World War I battle considered sacred in Australia. I really wanted to get to Gallipoli, as did Justin Langer. I told the ACB officials that I was prepared to buy my own ticket to Turkey to meet the team and see the place that is so meaningful to all Australians. No dice. They were keen to keep the squads apart and would not let us join the other guys at Anzac Cove. I remember feeling quite upset by this decision, but as I held myself responsible for not being in the one-day unit, I felt that it was partly my own fault.

So, despite some minor hassles, I thought I'd done the right thing by getting to England early. And even though I didn't bat particularly well in the early tour games, I was in reasonable shape when I went into the First Test at Edgbaston, in Birmingham, on 5 July.

And that was an amazing game. We won by an innings and 118 runs on day four, getting our Ashes defence off to a perfect start. In every detail except one, the first day was the ideal beginning to the summer's cricket. We were on top early, reducing England to 9 for 191 before Andy Caddick and Alec Stewart put on 103 runs, a record stand for the tenth wicket. But this created an unusual situation for me. When the opposition is nine out and you're the opening batsman, you start thinking about what you'll soon be doing at the crease. Once that final wicket falls, an opening batsman has ten minutes to be back out in the centre. A long last-wicket partnership like the one between Caddick and Stewart can try your concentration and sap your emotional strength. It's a bit like an endurance test for your nerves. It sure was for mine.

That long stand made me increasingly anxious. At one stage I was fielding on the boundary at fine leg and had trouble focusing on the pitch area – it all seemed blurry to me. Finally Stewart got out and I was back in the dressing room getting ready to bat, with about 90 minutes left in the day. By this stage, I was really struggling. My vision was still blurred and everything looked very strange and white to me. When I got back to the middle to face the first ball, I felt I was on the verge of being sick. But thankfully the experience of all those years opening the batting took over.

I took block from the umpire and looked down the pitch to see England's star bowler Darren Gough way back at the top of his run-up, rearing to go. The crowd was roaring, their faith in England restored by Stewart and Caddick's heroics. But I couldn't hear the noise. I rarely did when I was batting. I settled over my bat and looked towards Goughie and saw a familiar, yet blurred, sight. I couldn't focus on him at all. All I knew was that he was on his way, charging in at me with a new ball in his big paw. My Ashes series was about to start and I felt like I was in some kind of parallel universe. The struggle to end England's innings had allowed me way too much time to think about how big this tour was for me and my cricketing future. I knew my bat needed to do all the talking on this tour, given the doubts that were creeping in from the people around me. And now with the willow in my hand I knew what I had to do.

Goughie's first ball landed short of a length, well outside off-stump. It was the perfect ball to let go and give myself time to get it together – but it was also the ideal ball to square cut. Instinct took over. I smashed it through point for four and ended up tearing 17 off that first over. By stumps I was 76 not out off only 78 balls. I'd been quite shaky until I hit a straight on-drive back past Caddick. That's a hard shot to play at any time, so when you get one right you know you're playing well. I hit that ball for four and thought, *Okay, this could be a good day.*

I hadn't planned to bat so aggressively, yet it worked incredibly well. But I got out early the next day when I should have settled in to score a big hundred, which would have been the perfect start to the series. Instead of giving myself time, I blasted away and was dismissed. Still, we had already knocked the stuffing out of the Poms by the end of the first day. For a while, especially during that Stewart and Caddick stand, England thought they could match it with us, but by stumps we were totally in control. And the fact that I had attacked so hard emphasised that. At a press conference at the end of the series, Steve Waugh said that my innings had been one of the most significant factors of the whole series. But by the time he said that, I was already out of the team.

We walked all over the Poms in that First Test, and then moved on to Lord's, for the 19–23 July match, where I was out for 25 in the first innings. After my whirlwind first day at Edgbaston, this was a slow, hardcore, opener's innings. The pitch at Lord's was doing quite a bit – which suited England, whose new-ball bowlers were in good form. I was pleased that I worked hard at the crease for nearly two hours in trying conditions.

This innings was a sign of things to come. The pace

bowlers from both sides – Australia's McGrath (who got 32 wickets in the series) and Jason Gillespie, and Gough – had it all over the opening batsmen for most of the series. Matty Hayden, my partner for the four Tests I played, averaged just a little over 30; England's openers Michael Atherton and Marcus Trescothick averaged 22 and 32 respectively. The pitches were not very good and the new ball was really jagging about. I wasn't the only one struggling to make big scores. No opener from either side would make a hundred, at least not until the Fifth Test.

In the second innings at Lord's we only had to make 14 runs to win the match, so I went out and tried to be a hero. Bad move. I got out for 4 off five balls. I suppose that's a classic example of my attitude to batting. If I were only interested in my figures, I would have grafted a few runs and been not out at the end of the game, which really boosts your average. But that was never my approach to small chases. I preferred to go out and entertain, rather than playing safely and getting 20; and if I got out, so be it. Looking back at my career, I feel I scored enough of my good runs when they were really needed. I don't think you could ever call me a 'flat-track bully' – the type of batsman who makes big scores when the pitch is kind, the bowling kinder and the match already under control. In fact, I missed out on a lot of flat wickets during my playing days because I'd let my focus waiver. But I'm proud of the fact that when runs were needed – such as in that first innings of the First Test in Edgbaston in 2001 – I could really turn it on.

Stephanie arrived after the Lord's Test. I'd agreed that Steph should come to England so we could work on our marriage, but during an Ashes tour, that was a huge move on my part. I'm not really sure what I was thinking at the time, because those long, intense tours are hard enough on a healthy relationship, let alone one in need of repair.

There was still a lot more cricket to be played and I was determined to do well on the field. I was throwing myself into training, working hard to get my feet moving better while batting. Frankly, besides needing runs for myself, I knew that I could shut up the rumour-mongers if I was scoring heavily and doing my job. There has always been so much speculation about Shane Warne's off-field antics, but because he keeps performing so well as a player, he has stayed afloat. I felt I could divert attention from my personal life – and thereby buy time to work through my problems – by scoring a load of runs. The last thing I needed was a rumour that might brainwash one of the selectors into thinking I needed a break from the game. If I lost my hold on cricket I knew I would be in big trouble.

The domination of the opening bowlers continued through the first four Tests. It was bloody tough work facing the new ball, but my technical problem – my tendency to move across my stumps too early and too far – made it even harder for me. I was getting into the wrong position, with my head moving sideways when the ball was being released. Even though coach John Buchanan watched endless game videos, he didn't spot my fault initially until I pointed it out. (Or if he did notice it he didn't tell me.)

I just couldn't put my finger on what was different about my technique in England compared to the recent

Australian summer, where I'd batted really well with the same exaggerated initial movement. I was working overtime in the nets, hitting a lot of balls, but the problem persisted. There was no easy fix for this type of problem, which minimised my initial batting movement of back and across. It could take six hard months of work in the nets to eradicate. So I carried this technical fault into games in which the fast bowlers already had the advantage. The only batsman-friendly pitch was at the Oval, in south London, the venue for the Fifth Test on 23–27 August. But by then I'd been dropped.

At the same time, I learned that the rumours about me weren't isolated to within the team. There were whispers about me swirling around in Australia too, generated mainly by journalist Danny Weidler from Sydney's *Sun-Herald*. He had a gossipy back-page sports column where he kept having little digs at me. He loved opening his snippets along the lines of: 'The recently separated, tattooed, red-Ferrari-driving Michael Slater ...' These comments increased the rumours, which is why Stephanie joined me on the 2001 tour. I thought the best way to calm everything down would be to invite her to England and see how we got on together. It was a disaster. You just can't reconcile a troubled marriage on a cricket tour, especially when it's tough going, as it was for me both on and off the field, and your head's totally into cricket.

Even though Stephanie and I had been apart for a good few months, we were optimistic. We really hoped to sort something out. But things were very tense during her visit. Typically, when all is going well for me on the field, the rest of my life falls into place. Sadly, the reverse could also be true, which made this a really difficult time for both of us. Steph was only in the UK for a few weeks, but it didn't help our relationship.

I soon realised that I'd asked her to join me for all the wrong reasons. I should've stuck to my original plan and told her we'd meet up and talk when the tour was over. That would have been the sensible thing to do.

First, Stephanie caught up with a friend in France and arrived in the UK on 14 August, two days before the start of the Fourth Test at Headingley, in Leeds. Early in the game we went out for dinner with Dad and Claire. They'd come over as part of Dad's retirement holiday – he had always dreamed of following me on an Ashes tour. After the meal we came back and had a drink in the hotel, and I just knew everything wasn't right. I felt weak. I also felt that I'd let us both down by not being clear or speaking my mind about our marriage. I realised I was going to hurt Steph even more because she'd come all the way to England.

At one point, Dad and I were in the gents and I looked around and said to him: 'Dad, it's not working. I can't do it. I'm not happy and I know that this is taking my mind off the cricket, which I really need to focus on right now. I'm finding it really difficult.' I told him that I was going to ask her to leave.

His reply was something along the lines of: 'Well, you have to do what you have to do.' He's never been the kind of guy to give his kids strong advice. He's tended to leave it up to us, which is good – only this time I think I was hoping to hear something more decisive.

After dinner, I decided to let Steph know how I felt. We were in our hotel room when I told her it wasn't working out and I thought it would be better if she went home. It was a selfish decision, but I felt I needed to be selfish at the time, and it was extremely emotional for both of us. It was harder for Steph because she wanted to sort things out, and it had turned into a disaster. She couldn't understand my behaviour. But I was firm, so on the following day Steph drove to Lancashire, where she stayed with my uncle before flying back to Australia.

The next day I didn't speak to anyone about what had happened. It wasn't appropriate in the middle of a Test match and, frankly, I didn't think it was anyone's business. At that stage I didn't know that Steph had gone to the Gilchrists' room during the night, because I'd left our room after we'd talked. So the players probably knew more than I did about what had happened after I left the hotel the previous night. I tried to act normally, which was hard to do.

Adam Gilchrist was captain for that Fourth Test at Headingley, while Tugga recovered from a badly torn calf muscle. So the acting captain was now directly involved in my personal problems. The drama couldn't get any worse. And Gilly, understandably, would bring it up with Steve Waugh. It was a mess. And a few days later I was dropped from the Test side – forever.

All this came on top of an incident from a few days earlier, which in my view was not very serious, but it was a lapse in my behaviour that came at a bad time. Three days before the Fourth Test I went out to meet some friends from one of the tour's sponsors, who happened to be staying at the England team hotel. I had a few drinks there and returned to my room at about 12.30 am. Word got around very quickly that I'd been at the England team hotel. It was hardly a hanging offence; we had no curfew or strict rules, and it was left up to each player to do what he considered to be the right thing.

But the problem was intensified the next morning when I slept in and missed the bus to training. I hadn't set the alarm properly on my new mobile phone and I'd had a bad night's sleep, which was not unusual for me because of my AS. My room was dark and I had no idea what the time was. The phone rang at 10 am. It was our physio, Errol Alcott, telling me that everyone was downstairs waiting for me. I jumped out of bed and into some clothes, but by the time I got to the lobby the bus had left without me. Our policy was that the bus would wait for five minutes and if the late person had not appeared by then, it would leave without him.

I ended up getting a lift to training with one of the Australian photographers. We arrived at the ground just as the other players were going into the dressing room, so I didn't miss anything other than the bus. I walked into the dressing room with a bit of an attitude.

'Well, thanks for coming and knocking on my door, guys,' I said.

Ricky Ponting flew at me. 'You've made a mistake, Slats,' he said. '*You're* the one who's missed the bus, so don't come in here and blame us.'

Although my comment had been partly tongue-in-cheek,

I knew I was in the wrong and back-tracked straightaway. I didn't want to cause a stir.

'Look, I didn't mean that,' I said. 'Sorry. I know it was my fault.'

Ricky can be a cheeky bloke at times, someone who's always ready with a quip, so I didn't worry too much about what he said. But looking back, I realise I should've taken it as a sign that some of the guys were losing patience with me.

This was the first time in my career that I'd missed a bus to training, so I was pretty sheepish during the training session. Adam Gilchrist told me that my effort that morning was not good enough. I didn't have a problem with Gilly's comment, especially given he was captain and might've been feeling tense before the Test. But I didn't think it was a big enough issue to be raised in front of the whole squad. It felt as if he were belittling me.

A few minutes later we were all stretching near the fence and I was next to Adam. I said, 'Don't forget where you came from.' It didn't come out well, but I was trying to remind him that we'd known each other for a long time and had worked our way through cricket together, and that perhaps he could've treated me with more courtesy. He looked, listened, and said nothing.

That whole week in Leeds was an incident-packed nightmare. The ten-minute turnaround period before Matty Hayden and I went out to bat in the second innings of that Fourth Test summed up how unpredictable my world had become. I had a pretty regular routine when the opposition's tenth wicket fell. I'd acknowledge the key Australian bowlers from that innings then run off the ground, normally straight to the bathroom, where I'd wash my hands and face to freshen up. Then I'd change my whites if I was sweaty and put on my batting gear. The umpires ring the bell about two minutes before they want the first ball bowled, so you have about seven or eight minutes to get yourself mentally and physically ready to bat.

In Leeds I was ready to go, or so I thought, just as the umpires were on their way to the middle. Gloves on, I picked up my bat and reached for my helmet, which I always put in the same spot in my bag. It wasn't there. I was confused. I started to make a fuss, looking around, but without any luck. I then yelled out, 'Has anyone taken my helmet?'

'No,' was the reply from my team-mates.

So I had to borrow a helmet, which was a hassle because the protection grill was too close to my face and I had to unscrew it to alter its position – and this takes time. I could feel Steve Waugh watching me like a hawk. Matty Hayden was at the door waiting to go and now the entire English side was on the paddock. In my haste, I sliced open my finger on the grill. Blood was spurting everywhere. Tugga told Ricky Ponting to get ready quickly, because he might have to open with Matty.

'No,' I snapped. 'I'll be right.'

Errol had to perform an emergency bandaging job on my finger and eventually Matty and I made our way out to bat. I reckon we just made it and were on the verge of being 'timed out' by the umpires.

So what had happened to my helmet? A couple of days later Tugga brought up the helmet incident: he told me I was disorganised and lacked focus. But it turned out that Justin Langer, twelfth man for the Leeds Test, had mistakenly given my helmet to one of our close-in fielders when England was batting; the fielder had then brought it off the field but tucked it away at the far end of the dressing room, near Justin's kit bag. When I got out, I returned to the rooms still in shock about my helmet and cut finger. As if by miracle, there was my helmet sitting nicely where it should've been in the first place.

We ended up losing that Test at Headingley. Gilly made a fairly generous declaration, setting England 315 in the final innings and English batsman Mark Butcher made a brilliant 173 not out to win the game. After the match I was in the dressing room chatting to a few people. I commented that it had been an aggressive declaration, which was great for the game, and noted that we lost because England had batted so well, especially Butcher. I think this was a fair assessment of the game. Gilly either heard me say it or was told what I said, and took it as a criticism of his captaincy, as I later found out from Steve Waugh.

● ⑪ ●

After the Leeds match, we all travelled to London on the team coach to prepare for the Fifth Test at the Oval. It was always a good feeling to return to London, because the Royal Garden hotel in Kensington was our headquarters for the three-month tour and it was as close to a home as we had while in the UK. As soon as I checked in I was approached by Steve Bernard.

'Slats,' he said to me, 'drop your things off and come straight to Steve Waugh's room. He'd like to see you. I'll be there as well.'

I felt as if someone had punched me in the guts and I felt sick to the stomach. I knew exactly what I was about to hear: the skipper was going to inform me that I wasn't playing in the Fifth Ashes Test. My first reaction was to quit on the spot. I'd had enough of pretty much everything. For more than a year I'd been struggling with the break-up of my marriage and the various vicious rumours about me – and now this. It was simply too much to handle.

I dumped my bags, gulped back a glass of water, washed my face and took the lift up to Steve's room. My worst fear was about to become a harsh reality. I'd been dropped before, in 1996, and that kind of pain doesn't go away. As the lift climbed, my feelings changed from fear to anger. I resented the fact that no one in the team leadership group had made any comments about my so-so form (if they thought it was an issue). At no point during the 2001 tour had there been any kind of warning that my place in the team was under threat.

My behaviour on the tour had probably been fairly erratic, but given that my marriage was breaking up, that's not surprising. Yet during that long lead-up to my sacking, not one member of the squad's leadership had the guts or consideration to talk to me about my problems. And I didn't understand why my cricketing colleagues

Adam Gilchrist, Steve Waugh, John Buchanan or Steve Bernard hadn't pulled me aside if they thought I had some kind of conflict of loyalty when Gilly became captain for the Fourth Test. I knew my personal life was in free fall, but cricket was providing me with some necessary purpose and focus, and I felt my place in the Test side should be judged by my on-field performance alone – and nothing else.

And if statistics account for anything, I'd contributed plenty over the years. I'd played 74 tests, averaging over 40, a figure that most critics and players consider the benchmark for an opening batsman. I'd been one of only four players to be involved in every one of the side's world-record sixteen wins on the trot. I'd also like to think that my aggressive style of batting had put a few bums on seats all around the cricketing world. And I don't think that was just ego – I had the facts and figures to back it up. But there I was, angry and confused, knocking on Tugga Waugh's hotel-room door with the sinking feeling in my guts and heart that my Test career was about to end.

Steve looked nervous when he opened the door. He was shaking and spoke in an edgy, uncomfortable manner. Although I'd played a lot of big games alongside Steve, many with him as skipper, I'd never considered him much of a communicator, unlike his predecessor, Tubby Taylor. Steve's method of captaincy was all about action and leading from the front. Steve Bernard was also there, but he didn't say much. The team manager looked just as uncomfortable as the captain.

Tugga started by saying that he'd been concerned about

me for some time. He said that some of the things he'd noticed me doing – or not doing – had been damaging the team spirit. He also said that I'd been a negative influence on the team. As he talked, Steve was unable to maintain eye contact with me at all.

I was stunned. In the same way that no one had spoken to me about my form, no one had mentioned that I'd been damaging team spirit. I replied as soon as the words had left his mouth.

'Steve, I need examples, because this is the first time you've said *anything* like this to me. I'd like a chance to answer any accusations and tell you the real story, if there is something to defend, or to admit fault if that's the case.'

He mentioned various things, such as my sleeping in and missing the team bus before the Test in Leeds. He also mentioned another incident, in Somerset, when I had to do a photo shoot for the official Test magazine (which had been okayed by management) and the photographer had kept me waiting, so I was a couple of minutes late for warm-up. Team management had accepted this explanation, but it didn't seem that Tugga had.

Another thing Steve brought up was my work for Channel 4 during the one-day series, prior to the Tests. I hadn't been involved in the one-day games, so I thought this was perfectly okay, and I had permission from the ACB to do the commentary, of course. My take on working in commentary was completely different from Steve's. I thought the commentary gig was a perfect opportunity for me to stay involved with cricket during the off-season. It's a shame I couldn't have explained this to him earlier –

along with a number of other things – but I just wasn't given the chance. Steve said he got the feeling that I wasn't sure whether I wanted to be in the commentary box or on the field.

He then used the missing helmet saga as a so-called sign of my lack of organisation. I had the strong sense that Tugga was looking for excuses to get me out of the team.

Then Steve dropped the not-completely-unexpected bombshell: he said that he and Adam Gilchrist, who would be vice-captain for the final Test, felt that I should be 'rested' for the Oval match. He didn't say I was dropped, just that I was being rested. Anyone with a passing interest in cricket knows that there is a big difference between the two. Steve said it was all about giving me the time and space to sort out the issues he'd raised.

I completely disagreed – and I told him just that. Given everything else that was going on in my life, the game was giving me a focus. I told him that the last thing I needed was to miss a Test match.

'Steve, I hope this decision is based on form alone and not personal reasons,' I said to him, point blank, 'because this is the first time that you and I have discussed any of my personal issues. And I certainly haven't been trying to hide them from anyone. I've felt that I've been handling things okay. It would have been nice if you'd raised these concerns with me earlier and given me the chance either to explain myself or change my behaviour.'

Tugga finally came clean. He said that while my dropping was partly due to form, he added that he believed my personal life was the real problem and that I needed a break to sort it out. But I wasn't quite ready to accept what he told me. I reminded him that this had been a tough series for top-order batsmen on both sides. I also reminded him that this was the last Test match of the series and that the Oval pitch was the best for batting in the entire country.

'I know I'm not batting the best at the moment,' I admitted to him, 'and I know my foot movement is not at its peak, but I'm working hard. You know for a fact that I'm working overtime on my batting. I'm getting it right, I really think I am – but let's face it, the pitches have been very hard to bat on.'

Steve wasn't flinching, however. 'That might be so,' he replied, 'but we're sticking with the view that you need a break.' He added that he thought it was just a temporary thing – a rest, as he'd said earlier, not a dropping – and that he expected me to make it back into the first XI for the First Test in Brisbane against New Zealand, in November 2001.

There was no way Steve was going to back down. I was angry and frustrated, understandably. But clearly he wasn't ready to listen to my explanations. I stood up, turned around, and headed for the door – although I had one more thing to say to Steve.

'You're trying to play God here,' I said in parting. 'You haven't discussed anything with me before this or asked how I was going, and here you are, essentially sacking me from my job, without any kind of advance warning.'

Still shaking with anger, I reminded him of the strengths of the current Australian side, of the qualities that had led many people to liken us to Bradman's 1948 Invincibles. I suspected that he was sacking me, not resting me. And I knew how hard it was to regain a Test spot from that position.

'As much as you feel that this is a temporary thing,' I told him, 'you know how difficult it is in this side. It's such a tough side to get into that if someone new gets an opportunity, there's a good chance they'll do well. That's the way it is in the Australian team – it's not like other Test teams.' (Of course I had no way of knowing that day just how well my replacement, Justin Langer, would do. But that's history now.)

'And when you're telling everyone about the selection change,' I added, 'I'd like you to mention the real reasons why I'm not in the side. I think you need to let them know what's really happening. But as far as I'm concerned, you're trying to play God,' I repeated. 'You haven't asked me anything about all this until now and suddenly you're dropping me from the side. Well, stay on your high horse and continue to play God.'

With that I left his room.

I felt incredibly mistreated. Everyone knew the Oval pitch would be a belter, a world away from the slow, seaming tracks we'd had to deal with in the previous games. I thought I'd done enough with the bat to be given a final match on the best batting strip of the summer. It had been a tough series for the top-order batsmen – I was only averaging 24 to that point, but I'd played that key innings of 77 in the First Test. With no one else really vying for my spot, I thought I deserved the chance to finish the Ashes series with a big score on a decent pitch. But that would never happen.

Still stunned, I headed back downstairs, changed quickly and got ready for training. I wasn't exactly in the greatest mood as I sat on the bus on that twenty-minute trip to the Oval, and I didn't say a word. I was still fuming when we arrived at the ground and got into a huddle for a team chat. We talked about the Leeds Test and what had gone wrong. Then Steve Waugh announced that I was out of the team and Justin Langer was in. Hearing that Justin was replacing me was almost as much of a shock as the conversation in Steve's hotel room. Justin had never opened the batting – and he was having a horror tour, averaging less than 20 in the tour matches. He was in the worst touch of his career and hadn't looked like playing a Test. He was really feeling it too; there was no way he was in the right mindset to play in the Oval game.

I was amazed, frankly. I was a specialist opener and I felt that my replacement should be one as well. If anyone was going to take my place, I thought it should be Jamie Cox. He'd been batting well with Somerset and could easily be called up.

When Steve didn't explain why I'd been dropped, as I'd requested of him, I simply couldn't hold back.

'Stephen,' I said, 'tell the guys why I'm not in the side.'

Stubborn as ever, Tugga replied that I could explain if I wanted to, but he had no intention of doing so. I wasn't going to take this, so I snapped back at him, telling him I thought the other players had a right to know why I'd been dropped. My team-mates sat there, stunned, wondering what on earth was going on. At this, Adam Gilchrist had his say. 'Slats,' he barked, 'shut up. You're out of order; you're out of line. We're trying to get ready for the next Test match and this is not appropriate.'

Even though, admittedly, there was an element of truth in what he said, I'd never seen Adam react that way. I was so surprised that I decided to sit back and just let the tension defuse. After John Buchanan said a few words, we headed off for some warm-up laps.

Training was the last thing I wanted to do. I was shaking and crying. I could feel my blood pressure rising. I was completely gutted − I felt totally isolated. I had problems off the field and now my job had been torn away from me, and all without my having had the chance to discuss my situation with the skipper or vice-captain. So instead of training, I grabbed my gear and walked back across the ground and into the dressing room. I still can't believe I stormed away from training. It was a strong move, but I couldn't stop myself. I had to leave.

When I was halfway up the stairs I was stopped by Matty Hayden, who had always been a good mate and someone I respected very much. I was still crying, and I noticed that Matt was crying, too. He told me not to leave.

'I can't train today, Haydos,' I said. 'I can't do this. I need to go.'

So Matty went and finished his lap. When I walked into the dressing room, our support staff − the manager and assistant manager − were there. Understandably, they were surprised to see me. But there was simply no way I could train, not with all this negativity running through me. I felt completely alienated and rejected. Then Shane Warne walked in and put his arm around me.

He asked if I was okay and gave me a cigarette. 'Think about what you're doing, Slats,' he said. 'Don't do anything that can affect your future.'

I appreciated his concern but I knew I had to leave. So I walked out of the room, flagged down a taxi and headed back to the hotel. I was totally devastated and had no idea what I was going to do next. Eventually I went to a cafe on the King's Road in Chelsea, which had become my regular spot during the tour. I spent the afternoon there, having a few drinks and thinking about my life.

One person I did try to contact was my old team-mate Ian Healy, who was in England commentating and leading a tour group. Until his retirement in 1999, Heals had been my closest friend in the team. I knew he would've been a great guy to speak to, I could talk to Heals about anything. But he was tied up with his various commitments and we couldn't connect. That was a real shame, because I really could have used his advice.

So I sat there, feeling utterly alone. My marriage was as good as over, my team-mates thought I was going mad, and my Test career seemed at an end.

● ⑪ ●

That night, most of the team were going to a Madonna concert. Being such a music nut, I'd usually have been the first guy in the taxi, but not tonight. I just couldn't face it. So the guys went off without me.

We had another training session the next day and it went considerably better than the day before. I even had a chat with Steve and Gilly at the end of it and told them I would be okay for the Test. I'd calmed down and realised that they were the decision makers — and I couldn't do anything about it now. I knew that it was best to be a team man, and I'd always prided myself on being just that, rather than a selfish cricketer. I didn't want to make a bad situation even worse. I told my captain and vice-captain that I accepted their decision, even if I didn't agree with it, and that I'd be there doing my bit in a supporting role during the Test.

But it wasn't easy. I felt absolutely no ill will towards Justin Langer, but it was very, very hard to sit in the team room and watch him regain his form and his place in the side with a ton in perfect batting conditions. Everything that I'd predicted for the Oval — the flat pitch, the fast outfield — turned out to be true. We won the toss and racked up 4 (declared) for 641, with the Waugh twins scoring centuries as well as Justin. It was a total run-fest on a pitch that I knew would've helped me to regain my form and make a big score. But just as I had in England eight years earlier, Justin had grabbed his chance. It was the beginning of a golden stretch for him, which served to prove my point that being dropped from the Australian team, even for a so-called rest, could end a career — my career. I sat there watching and thinking about how Steve Waugh and Adam Gilchrist had created a fateful change in my career and Justin Langer's; one negative, the other positive.

It was significant that the 2001 tour was the last time that team selection was left to the vice-captain, captain and coach. From then on, there was always an official selector on tour, who would select the team in discussion with the vice-captain and captain. This came about as a direct result of my sacking, because Steve and Adam were so uncomfortable with the decision they felt they had to make. The rule of having a selector on tour is still operating in 2005.

Murphy's Law being what it is (as it operated against me through Langer's continuing success with the bat), not only did Justin score that hundred at the Oval, but he repeated the dose in the First Test against New Zealand a few months later, at the Gabba in Brisbane. His opener's spot in the team was secure, as was Hayden's – they'd put on 224 in Brisbane, following on from their stand of 158 at the Oval. It was the beginning of a beautiful friendship and partnership, and I was never going to play for Australia again.

I've never felt any bitterness towards Justin Langer. He was given an opportunity, he rose above the self-doubts he must've had at the time, and he kick-started his career. Good luck to him.

As for me, for five days starting on 23 August, I still had to get through that final Test match at the Oval – as a reserve. I was determined to stay involved in the team, but at a certain distance. It's incredibly difficult for any player who has been dropped. When you're in the team, even if you're struggling for form, you're still part of the action every day. There's a purpose to everything you do at practice because you know you're going to be out in the middle in a day or two. When you're dropped, everything can fall apart, and that's how it felt to me. But I realised that I had to hang in there. There was one week of the tour to go, and although I was very upset, I knew I had to keep it bottled up. Right now I had to think of the team and the Fifth Test match, to give it my best for a few more days and then face the rest of my career and life.

In the end, I was pleasantly surprised by how I handled that final Test. After the game, Tugga gave me another shock when he told me that he'd expected me to get on a plane back to Australia and leave the tour early. Now, *that* would have been a dumb move, one that would've definitely ended my career. All this proved was how much he misunderstood me, I think, and everything that was going on in my world. Tugga seemed to reckon that I'd either lost the plot completely or had never really been a committed, professional Australian cricketer. Either way, his instincts were wrong and it made me wonder what the others were thinking about me.

At the end of the Test I asked to speak to Steve and Adam Gilchrist. I was still in a very ordinary 'space'. I asked them straight up where all this left me.

'Whatever differences we've had,' I said, 'you felt the need to do what you did. And hopefully we can now move on and maybe I still have a future in this game.' I think by then they'd realised that my 'resting' hadn't really worked out as they'd anticipated — Justin Langer's making a century was hardly on the cards. Suddenly what had seemed a temporary omission to help me get my life back together had turned out altogether differently.

Misunderstood

Steve and Adam said they couldn't see why I wouldn't be back in the team for the First Test in Brisbane on 8 November. But I disagreed. As I'd warned Steve when he told me he was dropping me, no one took their place in the Australian team for granted – and you don't drop a player because he needs a break. The guys-in-waiting are always of the highest quality, good enough to seize the moment and stay in the team. And that's exactly what happened in my case.

Still, it was a reasonable enough conversation. It ended with their asking me what I was going to do now the tour was over. I wasn't sure what I'd do when I got back to Australia, but I did have a European holiday paid for and I told them I was going to take it. Originally I'd booked the trip for Steph and me, feeling that it would be an ideal finish to the tour, and a much-needed break for both of us. Tugga said he was heading straight back to Australia; Adam said that he and Mel were staying in England for a while. That was the end of our conversation.

Then there was the usual end-of-tour celebration at the hotel in Kensington, but I didn't participate. I did my own thing. I just didn't want to be around certain cricketing guys at that time. I'd lost a lot of respect for John Buchanan, for one, by the end of the tour. He's a highly qualified coach, sure, but he also talked himself up as a family man, a guy who knew how to treat individuals. John had the opportunity to help me, an established player in a tough personal situation, but to be honest I feel he simply gave me the brush-off. I wasn't sure what my relationship with Steve Waugh and Adam Gilchrist would be like after this tour, but I did realise that things would change, probably for the worse.

● ⑪ ●

I stayed on for a few days in London before heading off to Europe. On the day I was leaving I had a brush with the tabloid media that showed me again how rumours can spin way out of control. It was an experience that would repeat itself in various forms over the next twelve months.

I was checking out of the hotel when I heard strange mechanical noises nearby. I turned to see what it was and spotted a paparazzo taking photos of me. Then a journalist (of sorts) came up to me and asked if it were true that my wife had been sent home with two broken legs.

'Sorry?' I said.

'We heard you took to her with your cricket bat in your hotel room,' he said.

I laughed and said, 'Ah, no. Wrong.'

Then I jumped into the cab and told the driver to take off, as quickly as possible. I couldn't believe what had just occurred and how absurd the accusation was. I laughed in disbelief and tried to forget it, which was pretty hard.

My holiday was interesting but lonely. I went to Venice, Vienna and Prague – great cities but places I would have enjoyed a lot more if I hadn't been in such personal and professional strife. I tried to relax and chill out. I read a lot, mainly self-help books, and used the time to reflect on my marriage and how I was going to get through this period of my life.

I also used this holiday as an opportunity to stop taking my antidepressant medication, Effexor, which I was still using to control my anxiety. It had become a safety blanket more than anything and I'd been waiting for a decent break from the game to say goodbye to it once and for all. I had tried during the Indian tour, but suffered withdrawals. I was never comfortable taking the ADs and wanted to get them out of my life, partly because I felt certain people had played my AD usage against me. I also thought that if my behaviour *had* changed, then maybe this medication was the culprit. There was a hyperactive side to me – which I now know may be termed 'mania' – that I just couldn't explain.

This time around, the withdrawal was hell, and two days after taking the last of the ADs, I started getting bad withdrawals again. It felt like I was receiving electric shocks. These tingly surges would come on every ten minutes or so, and this kept happening for the next three weeks. But I got through them and was pleased.

I got back to London after the holiday to catch up with some friends for another fortnight or so before heading back to Australia. While I was there I took myself off to get some more tattoos. I already had the Superman emblem on my right shoulder, out of respect for my favourite group, Bon Jovi (I'd idolised them ever since first hearing their 1986 album *Slippery When Wet*), and I also had my Test player number, 356, tattooed on my right ankle. Justin Langer, Ricky Ponting and Mark Waugh also got tattoos of their Test numbers earlier in the tour. Now I wanted a Celtic symbol in the middle of my back and a Japanese emblem on my right shoulder.

I was booking myself into a tattoo place in Chelsea, and as I came out I ran into Mel Gilchrist. Adam, meanwhile, was across the road. Mel looked surprised to see me but said hello. I gave her a peck on the cheek and asked how she was. Gilly spotted me and it really looked like hard work for him to come across and say hello. He seemed to wonder why I was still in London.

Eventually Mel and Adam said something about their thinking that I'd gone straight home. I put them straight. I told them that I'd just come back from Europe and was spending a few days in London doing whatever. And then I jogged off. Later I heard that they were both floored that I was still in London and hadn't rushed home to talk to Stephanie.

Chapter 12

Wanted Dead or Alive

2001–2002

I didn't think it was possible, but after returning home from the England tour, things got even worse. Soon enough I was out of the NSW team, as well. It seemed that the NSW selectors were in agreement with the decision that Steve Waugh made in England: they also wanted to give me time to sort out my personal life. Fortunately, my dropping from the NSW team was handled in a much better fashion than my dumping from the Test side. John Benaud, the state's chairman of selectors and a former Test selector, pulled me aside and told me himself.

'We feel you need a break,' John confided. 'Your shot selection isn't good and we're worried that you're not doing your best.'

Benaud was someone I really respected. But at the time, with the media turning up the heat, his consideration didn't help much to make me feel better. I'd lost some focus as far as cricket was concerned, and I felt I'd been treated unfairly in England. So in the space of four months I had gone from representing my country to playing grade cricket for UNSW. It had been a swift, dramatic reality check – I'd hit rock bottom.

A lot of journos would phone me, trying to get a rise out of me. Once I was on the golf course and a journo (whose name I can't recall) called me on my mobile, asking if we could chat. I knew he was phoning from the press box at the SCG because I could hear all the background noise. When I asked his name, it seemed to be the same as that of the guy who'd written an article in the previous day's paper which had absolutely paid out on me. I asked if he was the same guy. When he admitted that he was, I snapped back, 'You're kidding, aren't you?' and hung up on him. Seconds later another journo called me. Obviously they were sitting together. I could almost visualise the guy smiling, as he was speaking to me in an incredibly patronising way. This time I didn't even reply, and hung up on him as well.

Typically, they wrote an article about how they'd tried to talk to me, detailing how aggressive I'd been in hanging up on them. And the calls just kept coming, as did my hanging-ups. It was becoming ridiculous.

At that time I had a unit in Rose Bay and the red Ferrari, which I guess was pretty hard to miss. One day, I was driving to my sister's house in Kellyville, in north-western Sydney, for a barbecue, with Natalie, a woman I was then seeing. When we got to William Street, coming through the tunnel under Kings Cross, the traffic was banked up at a red light. It was then that I heard a squeal of brakes to my left. Next thing I knew, there was a photographer running around the car taking photos. It took a few seconds for me to realise what was actually happening – it was like a scene in a movie where the paparazzi are going crazy. I'd experienced this back in the UK, but I simply didn't think this happened in Australia. When the lights turned green I was very tempted to clean him up, but by this time he was racing up William Street, trying to set up for another shot. I managed to duck into the inside lane and go straight down William Street instead of turning right. I didn't speak to Natalie for the rest of the 40-minute trip. It was all just too surreal.

After being dropped from the state team I missed the next club game because of a wedding. But to be honest, that incident with the photographer had made me feel even less like playing cricket. A week later I was finally back on the paddock, playing against North Sydney at the Village Green, the UNSW cricket ground. I was as nervous as hell. The media were there, including two or three photographers, so I felt like I was under a lot of scrutiny. I'd reached a very scratchy 12 when their fast bowler Aaron Bird dropped one in short. I tried to pull it but instead got clobbered on the helmet. The impact was enough to cut my eyebrow and there was blood everywhere, so I had to retire hurt. As I came off, I was thinking, *What else can go wrong?*

A lot, as it turned out. With blood streaming down my face, I looked around and saw cameras all over the place – Fox Sports over there, someone else here – and I turned to one of the cameras twenty metres or so away and said, 'There's a story for you, you pricks!' There was one photographer who got in my way as I tried to leave the ground. He stood directly in front of me and simply refused to move, shooting away while moving his lens closer and closer to my bleeding face.

After what had happened on William Street, this was just too much for me. I snapped, throwing my helmet and gloves at him. He said, 'What are you doing, mate?' but I didn't reply. I walked straight past him to the dressing room. I was using my four-wheel drive that day, and as I headed towards it he continued to take photos of me. He kept saying, 'You need to settle down, mate, you need to settle down.'

I turned around and said to him: 'Think about what you were doing back there. Do you think I want you in my face? You have *no understanding* of my situation. Put yourself in my shoes and see how you react.' I then got into my car and drove away.

Looking back, it was another case of my being pushed too far and reacting in an overly sensitive way. Some people have the ability to keep their emotions under control, but if you get poked enough, there's going to be a point at which you explode. I doubt there'd be many people who wouldn't have lost it, given the circumstances of that day – I just wish I hadn't done it in such a public way. I suppose that the game was seen as a comeback, so the media were watching closely. They, and the few officials at the ground, got more than they bargained for. I was just so vulnerable. At least the episode gave Aaron Bird, a young up-and-coming fast bowler who'd bowled the bouncer at me, some kind of profile, which I was pleased about. But the day had not played out in quite the way I would've liked.

I did finally get back into the state team for the last game of the season. It was a bizarre situation. I'd been dropped, but was then reinstated — as captain! Shane Lee had been the captain that year but he was injured. All the Test players were busy elsewhere, and I'd been scoring some good runs in grade cricket.

But we lost against Tasmania in two days. It was frustrating because I always thought that captaincy was something that brought out the best in me as a cricketer, but I just didn't get much of a chance to prove it at first-class level. I think if I'd been offered the job earlier, it would've helped me to keep going. They should probably have then offered the state captaincy to Mark Waugh before he retired, but instead they gave it to Simon Katich. And he did a great job, leading NSW to victory in the one-day ING Cup and Pura Cup double that year, so I guess the selectors felt they'd made the right decision. But NSW cricket would have got a lot more out of the brilliant Mark Waugh if he'd had the added responsibility of the captaincy.

● ⑫ ●

As for my problems at the time, they still weren't restricted to the field. Most of the guys used managers to help negotiate their deals. I'd been managed by a company called Promotional Partners, a marketing promotions group to whom I was referred in 1993 following the first Ashes tour. I'd later signed up with Harry M. Miller's management company, in the mid 1990s. He had a big reputation as a tough negotiator and I felt it was worth a go to have a consummate professional managing my affairs.

While Harry always oversaw everything and got involved with the bigger negotiations, I also had a day-to-day contact in the office, who helped keep my diary and maintained good relationships with my sponsors. The people in these assisting roles seemed to change quite often. Just before going on the 2001 Ashes tour a woman from the office, whom I'd rather not refer to by name, had taken over my account. Initially, I thought she was outstanding. There'd been a heavy staff turnover at Harry's and to have such an enthusiastic person looking after me was a real bonus. Her attention to detail was great and it made for a terrific few months.

I then decided not to renew my contract with Harry, feeling that I should take on more responsibility in my life and start looking after my own affairs. Harry had been a fantastic manager, but there was a lot changing in my life and this was just another change I felt I needed to make at the time. Although this woman was no longer working for Harry M. Miller by the time I arrived home from England, she stayed in touch with me and, without my knowing it, continued to act as if she were managing me. She convinced a whole range of people – from my family and friends to sponsors and businesspeople – that she was still my manager. Her behaviour was very strange, and when we spoke I couldn't work out if she was telling the truth or inventing things. Initially she seemed like a lovely, caring, very capable person, so at times I found myself confiding in her about my personal life. But there was an obsessiveness to her that started to scare me. I couldn't quite work her out.

It got really out of hand, so I tried to sever my ties with her. She started to do some incredibly odd things. She would cruise up to car dealerships that she knew I had dealings with and borrow cars on the strength of my name, insisting that she was just going for a test drive. She returned one Mercedes after three weeks, dented, and the dealership then received a pile of parking tickets. It was while commentating in the UK that I realised this was happening. One of my mates, Bevan Clayton, who'd help me buy and sell a few cars, emailed me to ask if this person was still managing me as she said she was. I told Bevan that I didn't have anything to do with her anymore. It was then that he told me what had been going on. I started to wish I were still on board with Harry – he was great in tough predicaments and understood damage control inside out.

In my situation with the media, I'm sure Harry would have advised me to speak to certain journos, to get my side of the story out there, at least. But now I just clammed up, as the rumours started to build in the press about my 'going off the rails'.

It seemed people's minds had been made up when I bought the Ferrari, a purchase I made during the two-month period between the tour to India and the 2001 Ashes tour. There were so many negative connotations that seemed to be attached to that car. But what many people didn't realise is that I'd always had my heart set on being the proud owner of a gleaming red Ferrari at some stage in my life. I have to admit the timing of my purchase sucked, given the dramas of my life on and off the field, especially with my marriage, but with each day feeling like my last, I wanted to have the Ferrari experience sooner rather than later. So that's exactly what I did!

Although no mention was made of drugs at the time by the press, I knew that the rumours were out there. It was like the Steve Bernard–Malcolm Speed drama all over again. I'd now moved to a flat in Bondi, which I was sharing with Corey Richards, a batsman for both Bankstown and NSW. One night, Corey's mother called in tears, saying she'd just heard that I had a cocaine problem. She then said how worried she was for me and for Corey, who was sharing a house with someone with a 'drug problem'. Thankfully, Corey reassured her, telling her that she didn't need to worry; he'd been living with me for a month now and there was none of that going on.

But the trouble with this woman still persisted. I felt that so much of my life was spinning wildly all around me, and the last thing I needed was someone like her going behind my back and causing more trouble for me. I told her to get out of my life, but she simply wouldn't listen, she wouldn't let go. She not only called Steph, but also phoned people like Allan Border and Mel Gilchrist. I was never able to find out exactly what she was saying about me, but I assumed it was based on the usual rumours.

One day, an upset Steph called me to ask who this

woman was that kept phoning her. Soon after, my former team-mate David Boon rang to say he would be in Sydney soon and we should catch up. Then Ian Healy called and said he'd also be in Sydney at the same time, staying in the same hotel. I thought, *Great, two old mates whom I love and admire to death are dropping by and we're going to catch up.* It was just what I needed.

The night before I was due to meet up with them, I got a call from my brother-in-law Stephen.

'Mate, I feel bad about this,' he told me, 'but the reason I'm calling is to tell you that [the woman] has been on the phone to us every day this week. The first thing she said to Tracey was that she knew that you and Tracey come from a dysfunctional family.'

Stephen then told me that it was this woman who had organised the get-together with Boonie and Heals. She'd also asked Stephen, Tracey and Stephanie to come and meet me to help sort out my life – to stage an intervention, in short. Stephen had informed her that if she and Stephanie turned up to a meeting, I'd walk out, and he was right. I wanted to see my two cricketing mates, and I trusted my sister and brother-in-law. If Boonie and Heals wanted to ask me some questions about how I was doing, then fine, but there was no way I'd cop it if this woman was there trying to run the show. And I saw no point in involving Steph, either.

By this stage, I knew that our marriage wasn't working – and that it wasn't going to work. The blow-up on the 2001 England tour proved that Steph and I just couldn't be together anymore, although we maintained a good enough relationship and talked on the phone quite often. I'd started seeing Natalie, and was trying to move on with my life and rise above all the recent turmoil.

I really appreciated Stephen's call. It was a decent and loyal thing for him to do. I then called Boonie and asked him what the hell was going on. He admitted that it was the same woman who had phoned him. I told him that I still wanted to see him and Heals, but not her and Stephanie. He accepted that.

Not surprisingly, I went to the hotel feeling nervous and angry. Tracey and Stephen, however, seemed more nervous for me and were upset that I'd been dragged into such a meeting. Boonie did most of the talking. He said that everyone was concerned about me — there'd been rumours that I was drinking too much and that I might have been using drugs. Everyone said that if these rumours were true, they'd be prepared to help me out. (I later found out that they'd gone as far as to arrange an appointment for me with Dr Robert Hampshire, a well-known psychiatrist, and had booked me into the Golden Door, a health retreat on the Gold Coast.)

I told them that yes, maybe I had been drinking too much, but I wasn't an alcoholic. My drinking was confined to social occasions and I had no problem stopping at one or two. If I thought I had a problem with booze I'd seek help. But, I added, I was now a single guy and I was going out and enjoying myself. I guess I was catching up on missed opportunities. I had plenty of friends in the cricket world and when I went out with them for a night I might go at it fairly hard. But I also went for days without a drink.

'Guys, remember that I've just split from my wife,' I told them. 'And like most people who go through a marriage break-up, I'm letting off some steam and enjoying my new freedom. I might be partying a bit hard but I haven't gone off the rails, believe me.'

As for the drug rumours, I told them the whole story, how this had been based on innuendo and misunderstanding. I really got hot under the collar, as I'd heard this whisper far too many times. I told them I just didn't want to hear any more of this crap – *I did not do drugs*.

I'm really not sure what everyone thought after this meeting. I think they wanted to believe me but still had a few doubts about how I was coping. I know that they were acting out of kindness and friendship. Having spent some quality time with Ian Healy recently, I asked him what he was feeling after our get-together that day.

'I walked away comfortable with what you said and believed you 100 per cent,' he said, which was what I really needed to hear. It felt great to know that at least one of my closest friends believed in me at just about the lowest ebb of my life.

Eventually time passed and the woman drifted out of my life. But while it was happening I was seeking legal advice, asking about an AVO and that kind of thing, because she really was squeezing herself into every corner of my life and causing so much unnecessary trouble. It was a horrifying thought that behind my back she'd been calling people close to me and saying all sorts of stuff.

There was one other very strange encounter I had at that time, which was one of the more bizarre things that happened to me during my cricketing life. After the 2001 Ashes tour, I knew I had a fair bit of work to do to get my life back together. I was out of the Test team and winning back that spot was on the top of my to-do list. Then there was my shattered reputation to contend with, not just in the cricket world but also in the eyes of the wider public, and all those crazy rumours – whispers about my excessive drinking, my alleged drug use, my 'dodgy' heart, my depression, my erratic behaviour. I thought only Hollywood superstars had to deal with that kind of tabloid nonsense. And just when I figured the rumours couldn't get any more far-fetched ...

Stephanie rang to tell me that someone had called saying that there was an email about me doing the rounds. The email suggested that the reason I'd been dropped from the Test side was that one night during the Fourth Test in Leeds, Stephanie had stormed into the Gilchrists' hotel room at three o'clock in the morning demanding to know whether I was having an affair with Mel Gilchrist, and – get this – whether I was really the father of their as-yet-unborn baby. The email said that once Gilly found out I was the father of the child he made sure I was dropped from the side.

I was so shocked at first that I couldn't believe it. It was so absurd it was laughable. I mean, it had to be a joke. During the next week I had dozens of phone calls from family and friends, who had all read or heard about the email. Tracey and Stephen rang a few times, and they were in a terrible state. Stephen had received the same email and said it was really awful. Once I realised how widespread this rumour was I began to take it more seriously. The cruelty of it was astonishing. I sank into a real mental decline. When was I going to get a break? What had I done to deserve this shit?

I was in Sydney at this time and retreated from normal life as much as I could. I just didn't want to see anyone, anywhere. I spent my days locked up in the unit I was renting in Bondi. I was waiting for Gilly, or a team-mate or two, to call. Perhaps I should've called him and Mel immediately, just to let them know that we were all in it together. It was a terrible slur on Mel's character as well as mine, and must've been very hurtful for them both.

This vicious rumour proved to me that my life was way out of my control. A long list of minor matters had been blown out of all proportion by misunderstandings, malicious rumours and a simple lack of communication. My character had been questioned to such an extent that people now seemed to think I was capable of cuckolding a team-mate, a guy I'd known as a friend and player for years. The last straw was those calls from Stephen and Tracey – it seemed that even people whom I trusted and loved were questioning my character. When it was brought up at a family get-together one day, I stormed out. It was just too much to handle.

The Gilchrists decided to take legal action against the author of the email, and that was when this cruel prank was traced back to an English cricket website. Apparently, the people who ran the site sat around the office one day, clearly with nothing better to do, and tried to dream up theories explaining why I'd been dropped (because they were as puzzled as I was by my sacking). It seems they wrote their theories on a whiteboard, including the outlandish one about my alleged affair with Mel. Someone saw this and thought it'd be fun to send it out as an email. All I can say is that some people have a very twisted idea of a good time.

I was so dumbfounded by it all that I didn't even respond to an email from Gilly's manager, Stephen Atkinson, telling me they were suing the site. I had so many other things on my mind already that I just couldn't face this latest setback. I didn't have the energy to cope and just tried to turn my back on it. It took six months before I contacted Atkinson and took my own successful legal action. The money I received did little to compensate for all the pain, but at least it was some kind of payback.

At the time, I felt like someone who'd been wrongly accused of a horrible crime – of rape or murder. I was totally innocent, but, as they say, mud sticks. My only hope is that over time people will dismiss it as the stupid, thoughtless and hurtful rumour that it was. All I could do now was to get my life back on track, behave well in whatever I was doing and eventually convince people that I was a decent human being. And that was going to take some work.

Drinks Break

In the Booth

It's funny how the commentary opportunity that came my way in April 2000 has developed into something that I love and is now, for the most part, my job. I will always be grateful to Gary Francis at Channel 4 for taking a punt and giving me my first 'proper' commentary stint. At the time, those English summer months spent behind the microphone gave me a much-needed break from the negative publicity that was circulating in Australia. England soon became my safe haven.

Just like cricket itself, television is a tough industry that doesn't tolerate a lack of talent or commitment. I'm proud of the fact that while certain people in Australia thought I was off the rails, Channel 4 successfully employed me during four of the toughest years of my life.

I found with commentary, the hardest thing to get used to initially was the earpiece you wear, which allows you to hear and communicate with the director, who's calling the camera shots that are beamed into people's living rooms. The executive producer can also speak to you in this way while you're on air. It took me a few days to feel comfortable speaking on air while hearing voices in my ear at the same time, which can be quite distracting. But fortunately the first team I ever worked with – the

Channel 4 crew — was one of the slickest, most professional groups I've ever been part of. The director, Rob Sherlock, was one of the best in the business, and via my earpiece he'd feed me great ideas that I could incorporate into my commentary.

When I got to England in May 2000, Richie Benaud was one of my colleagues, along with Mark Nicholas, Barry Richards, Dermot Reeve and Ian Bishop. I had a couple of experiences in the booth with Richie Benaud that summer that are, in hindsight, pretty funny. At the Old Trafford Test I was more nervous in the box than I'd ever been out in the middle. After all, this was Richie Benaud, the doyen of cricket broadcasting. I was trying so hard not to stammer that I was hardly saying anything, and I certainly wasn't making any strong connection with the great man. We were both sitting on chairs that looked more like bar stools, and my feet were about twelve inches off the floor. About halfway through our 30-minute shift, things started to happen on the ground and wickets were falling everywhere. I started to get a little more animated, and every time something big happened, I'd leap to my feet. In one six-ball over, this happened two or three times.

What I didn't know was that Richie was wearing a long earpiece, with a cable that ran down past my chair. Every time I stood up I'd tread on the cable, tugging Richie's head savagely, again and again. But because I was looking at the play, I didn't notice what was going on. When I stood up for the third time, Richie's head slammed down on his left shoulder — and then he slapped me on my shoulder. Off mic, he said to me: 'Michael, if you do that again, you'll rip my head off.' I turned around and all the assistants and crew in the booth were pissing themselves laughing. I didn't speak again during that shift.

Later on in the same series, during the Lord's Test, we were watching a replay of a ball that almost bowled a batsman. 'That was terrific bowling,' I declared. 'It just about snuck under the bat.' I then turned to Richie and asked him whether the English audience would fully understand the word 'snuck'. (Aussies use it all the time, but I was sure we would struggle to find it in the *Oxford Dictionary*.) At first Richie didn't say anything, but about 20 or 30 seconds later, he said off air, 'I know of a few "ucks", Michael, but "sn" isn't one of them', before going straight back into the commentary. Again, all the crew fell about laughing.

Each stint on the microphone runs for 30 minutes and you are either the 'lead' or the 'colour' commentator. The lead calls each delivery as it happens and generally controls the commentary, while the colour or 'expert' calls the replays and tends to consider the more analytical side of the game. These are the general principles, but they vary depending on the rapport you have with your co-commentator, and on their own personal style.

Just as you are on the field, you're part of a team in the commentary box and work in a partnership each time you're on the air. And just like batting partners, some guys are easier to work with in commentary than others. I really enjoy being on air with someone with whom you can have a good conversation and a bit of banter. When it works well you almost forget that you're sharing your views with over a million viewers. I believe that the more interesting and insightful your conversation is, the more appealing it will be for the viewers.

I've built up a good rapport in the booth with another former Test opener, Englishman Michael Atherton, which I feel is due to our both being guys who talk openly and have fun on air. The amazing thing is that 'Athers' and I were committed opponents for years during various Ashes series – and now we're playing on the same team. Although we both opened the batting for our country, we had completely different approaches and attitudes to playing. Athers was a steady accumulator of runs, whereas I took a more aggressive approach to batting. He has often called me a 'slogger', to which I happily reply, 'You block artist!' Yet because of this difference in approach we have a great rapport and work well together on air. Hopefully the viewers also enjoy our different viewpoints and the occasional anecdote that we throw into the mix.

When we were in India in late 2004, Athers couldn't believe that a number of the Australian batsmen were 'walking', rather than waiting for the umpire's call on an appeal. 'I never thought I'd see the day,' he said to me, on air. 'Aussies are becoming *pussy cats* on the cricket field.' He then looked at me and said, 'I think we now have a big chance of winning the next Ashes series – you guys have turned soft!'

It's a lot of fun working with ex-players – and legends – from all eras and all countries. After a stint with Athers, I might be teamed with the great Indian batsman Sunil Gavaskar or English batting legend Geoffrey Boycott, the Indian all-rounder Ravi Shastri or West Indies star bowler Michael Holding, Mark Nicholas or the iconic Richie Benaud. I consider myself blessed to be working with these great people – and I can't help but learn fast in their company.

Soon after I started calling the game I realised that it's crucial to keep a constant eye on the pitch, even when you're not on air. Test cricket ebbs and flows – it can be turned on its head in one over – so you need to have a good feel for how the game is evolving. You not only have to observe the game but also predict the tactics that the captains and players might adopt. Generally, in a half-hour stint I'll have two or three points I'll want to get across, although these might be thrown out early if the game suddenly changes or your co-commentator takes a completely different path. Regardless, it's important to have an idea of where you want to go with your call.

Having said that, however, the way I commentate is also a little like the way I batted: I really try to capture the emotion and energy of the game and communicate it. The last thing I think the viewers want to hear is a boring, repetitive drone coming out of their TV. It's a challenge to keep the call lively, particularly when the contest is one-sided.

Recently, while in New Zealand for the Australian Test matches, I found it quite difficult to maintain a balanced view-point. Everyone knew the Aussies were going to win, which they did — convincingly, to the tune of three–zip. People actually started to bet not on who would win the game, but on how long the Aussies would take to do it.

In commentary, I think it's important to have a strong opinion about something, as long as you give this belief clear definition. It also really helps to be able to explain your logic. While the viewers may not necessarily agree with you, if they know where your point is coming from, you might offer them something to think about. Channel 9's Ian Chappell is a well-known and highly regarded commentator, someone from whom I have learned much in the few times we've worked together. I admire his willingness to voice a strong opinion — and he always explains himself well, never leaving you unsure as to how he arrived at his view. He has an incredibly deep knowledge of the game, too, and will always offer his views and yarns to those who share a similar love of and interest in cricket.

Speaking of strong opinions, one of the biggest challenges I currently face is speaking about the Aussie players with whom I've been team-mates, guys such as Shane Warne, Damien Martyn, Matthew Hayden, Adam Gilchrist and Glenn McGrath. It can be tricky, and I would never want to upset anyone, but because it's my job to call the game I won't shy away from calling it as I see it, however strong my opinion may be. Again, I guess as long as I explain my logic, and my criticism is constructive, not destructive, then that's just part of my job.

Clearly, it's still early days for commentating and me, but I realise that just like playing, it will take enormous dedication and work on my part to last in this industry. I really admire Richie Benaud and the way he has lived his life for so many years, spending six months in Australia commentating for Channel 9, and then six months in the UK working for Channel 4. Richie has an absolutely head-over-heels love for the game. I often think to myself, *How amazing must his life be?* I would love to forge a similar path one day.

It all starts with a dream, and someone like Richie proves that it can be achieved. For me, it's now about being head down and bum up – I know that hard work really can pay off. Most of all, it's fun having a new challenge. I'm loving it.

Chapter 13

I'll Sleep When I'm Dead

2002–2005

The 2002/03 domestic season had ended really well for me after I'd scored a double century in Western Australia and a century in the Pura Cup final against Queensland. I really felt that I was back on the selectors' radar – that there was a glimmer of hope that just maybe I could make it back into the Test team. I knew how unpredictably things could turn out. I'd witnessed it myself when I got into the Test team in 1993, at a time when everyone was tipping Matthew Hayden to make the first XI. And not long before he'd been chosen in my place in England in August 2001, Justin Langer had been in a bar in Brighton, crying, unsure if he'd ever play Test cricket again. Then he went and blazed away and secured himself a spot in the Aussie Test XI, a position he still holds. I've always believed that if your energy is good and you're training well, things can work out for you. And that's exactly how I felt at the start of the 2003/04 season.

So I had big hopes for the summer and I was working hard to prove that I still had the right stuff. I figured that even if I got back for just one Test match (which would have taken my career total to 75), I'd have been incredibly proud. So I was training hard and felt fit and strong, but I was overdoing it. After making a good 40 in NSW's opening game at the SCG, I headed off for our first tour of the season and this was when I started feeling ill. As it turned out, it was the beginning of the end of my playing days.

The tour took us first to Tasmania for a four-day match and then to Adelaide for a Pura Cup match, which was followed up by an ING one-day game. We were going to be on the road for two weeks. But during the first game, against Tassie, I felt really off colour. We'd had a team lunch the day before and I'd got on the red wine with spin bowler Stuart MacGill, which didn't help. I'd gone to bed early, but because I'd had a few drinks I woke up the next day feeling seriously disappointed with myself and my preparation, which wasn't as solid as it should have been. So even though I was ready for a big game, I was feeling a little bit seedy. I scored a hard-fought 20 or 30 in difficult conditions, but I felt out of sorts for the remainder of the game.

The first sign of what would eventually be diagnosed as reactive arthritis was a pain I felt at the base of my ribs, near my spine. It was around a cartilage or tendon area, and seemed typical of the pain I experienced when I had flare-ups of my AS. I immediately started having my AS treatment, as I'd done many times before whenever a flare-up occurred, but this seemed bigger than a typical AS outburst. I was feeling dizzy and nauseous, and my right ankle was swollen at the end of the day's play, which was unusual. When I got to South Australia my body was deteriorating. My ankles and knees were swollen – I'd never encountered such fluid in my ankles before – and my back was getting really bad. I knew something terrible was going on with my body.

It seemed that with every new day my health declined a little more. It was worrying me and making it hard to focus on the cricket I was there to play. The selectors were unsure at that time whether I should still be playing in the state one-day team. I ended up batting at number six, and when I came in, the game was close to lost. I reached double figures (16, I think) but was dropped for the next ING Cup match, days before my arthritis fully took hold.

By the time I got back to Sydney, my health had rapidly faded. I'd wake up with progressively worse swelling in my ankles. In fact, my right foot was now so swollen and painful that it felt like it had a heartbeat in it. I swear that at times, if there had been a hacksaw or axe in the house, I would've chopped off my foot – the pain was so bad. It was becoming a struggle to walk around and even getting out of the unit was difficult, because negotiating the stairs was just too big a challenge. So I stayed inside watching the world go by from my balcony.

I placed a call to Dr Ken Crichton, who had been helping me manage my AS throughout my career. During an acute bout he would work closely with my NSW team physio, Patrick Farhart, and if things got out of control, he would then refer me to a rheumatologist. Ken realised straightaway that something major was going on and referred me to the rheumatology department at Royal North Shore Hospital, where I immediately started treatment to try to control what had become a raging, out-of-control monster.

Typically, the initial treatment for AS was oral medication only (anti-inflammatory and steroidal tablets), but because of the acute nature of this condition they prescribed steroidal intravenous drips, one administered every other day for a week. It was a drastic measure, but if successful it could settle things down very effectively. The objective was to suppress my immune system, to stop it from running riot trying to fight alien bugs in my system that were not actually there. This is why my joints were so inflamed – my immune system was flooding them with white blood cells to fight infection (AS is an auto-immune disorder). The IV drips seemed to work for eight to twelve hours but then, bang, the inflammation would be back, bigger and even more horrible than before.

It got to the point where I just couldn't walk. On a few occasions I had to crawl to the toilet. So, following another sleepless night, full of the most amazing pain I'd ever felt, with my foot the size of a football, I was admitted to Royal North Shore. After a few days of theorising (and speculating), I was diagnosed with reactive arthritis, which is similar to AS but tends to be more acute initially and can be triggered by many different things. Anything from intense stress, food poisoning, a viral infection, or simply being run down can set it off.

The treatment is almost identical to that for AS, although the difference for me was that Prednisone, the drug that would normally curb my AS, wasn't working. I was petrified: would I be able to walk again, or live any kind of normal life? My only relief during the days in hospital was to fall into a wheelchair and wheel myself outside for an hour or two. If I were lucky, Jo Lobban, my new girlfriend (and now my fiancée), would be visiting so I'd have a driver, of sorts, to steer me around. Jo helped me take my mind off my troubles for a while, because she took such a daredevil approach to her wheelchair work and would whiz me around the hospital corridors, scaring the hell out of me!

As well as the treatment I've mentioned, my system was being flooded full of intravenous antibiotics. It was all guesswork really, and I felt like a human guinea pig; but with all the pain, I was willing to try anything. I wasn't thinking about playing cricket at this stage, I just wanted to get out of the wheelchair and walk again. I ended up spending ten days in hospital leading up to Christmas 2003 and probably should've been there a little longer, but there was just no way I was spending Chrissie in hospital.

What made this strange situation even stranger was that I'd really only just started my relationship with Jo. We met at an *Inside Sport* function at the Establishment, in Sydney, late in 2003. It was a fluke, because we both weren't going to go to the event, but at the last minute I'd decided that I should get out a bit more. We met towards the end of the night and locked into a fairly deep conversation that went on for about an hour and a half. After that we kept bumping into each other. Jo was rowing surfboats for the North Bondi surf club, so we started catching up for breakfast most Saturdays. After about a month we were seeing each other more regularly. It was a really nice, gradual build-up to our relationship. And because Jo works in public relations, she understood how the media could fuel incorrect and misplaced perceptions of people – especially me! She wasn't letting the warped public perception of me intrude on her own take. That was great and a pleasant relief.

Jo's an intelligent, professional and independently minded woman. She's also very sporty – she's as fit as. We have a lot in common, so it seemed very natural for us to get together. We could talk forever.

By the time I was admitted to hospital we'd been seeing each other for about two months. Our relationship had heated up. We'd both realised that we were right for each other. I remember leaving for that two-week road trip down south to Tasmania and South Australia, just before my arthritis kicked in, thinking that I didn't want to go. I wanted to stay in Sydney with Jo. But when I got back, as sick as a dog, it became a full-on challenging experience for both of us. Here Jo was: she'd met this new guy and now he was a cripple; we'd had an amazing time together before this, and then I was in a wheelchair and virtually helpless. I can't believe Jo saw it through. Her patience and understanding was amazing. Still is.

But my continuing ill-health did take its toll on our

relationship. For months Jo tried to work full-time, row competitively and look after me, both physically and psychologically. Then when I started to recover, we actually had a break for a month or so because it had taken so much out of her – and I'd been hard work. But Jo was phenomenal. I'd gone through a really deep depression at the time and I truly felt worthless as a human being. I felt an intense insecurity about being so helpless, given that my career was in jeopardy, and everything that goes with that. Jo's surfboat rowing meant she was off training and competing on the beach surrounded by all these fit strong guys, so it was hard to take. I don't think there's any way *I* would have stuck it out with me at that time!

Jo wasn't the only one who found my debilitating situation hard going. Dad and Claire came up one weekend to see me and were shocked by the state I was in. They were devastated by what this thing was doing to me and how much weight I'd lost, as were Mum and Barry, who also visited. I remember being put on one of those steroidal IV drips, and I was seated in a recliner chair in the chemotherapy ward. I'd lost over ten kilograms and looked pale and ill, and I was surrounded by cancer patients. When my hour-long treatment had finished, I walked out with Mum and Barry – though it was more of a shuffle because I had trouble moving my feet. I later found out that as they watched me struggle to my car, they both burst into tears. It was a terrible time for everyone.

There was no noticeable improvement for a long period, although I kept hoping that the new day would bring some relief or a little sign of improvement. I was on some crazy drugs, including a cancer treatment drug (Methotrexate) also used by arthritis sufferers in smaller doses. Reading the leaflet about the possible side effects alone freaked me out and made me think more than twice about using the drug. But I was desperate; I couldn't walk. And I was mentally low. It was like being at the bottom of a well – occasionally I'd catch a flicker of light but I couldn't see or feel any excitement about anything. It wasn't until April 2004, about four months after my arthritis set in, that the light started to flicker a little brighter and things started to get just that little bit easier for me.

During this time I was thinking a lot about my career as a first-class cricketer. As I've said, I had been really keen to have a strong season, so I'd put a lot of effort into training hard. I'd been optimistic that if I could score some good runs, maybe there was a chance of proving that I still had what it took to play for Australia, at the age of 33. My illness during the end of 2003 and early months of 2004 threw a massive spanner into the works. And I had all these questions running through my head: *What am I going to do if I can't play? What is the next stage for me?*

● ⑬ ●

I'd spent the last four English summers commentating for Channel 4 and had really enjoyed it. I felt I was doing okay at my second profession. I was really comfortable calling the game and loved being able to deliver some insight to the viewers – I really tried to bring the game to life for them. Perhaps the next stage of my life, when I would move on from playing cricket, was going to come sooner than I might have expected. In early February 2004, I received an unexpected call from Steve Norris, who works for Ten Sports out of Dubai. He wanted to know if I was available to cover the Australian tour to Sri Lanka the following month. I said that I'd love to do it. But I agreed to this on one of my good days – and the next ten were terrible.

I was struggling to walk or sit in the same position for very long. And I was in hospital every week, seeing my rheumatologist, who'd give me a blood test and check my blood count. I knew in my heart that I probably wasn't ready or well enough to take the risk and head to Sri Lanka, which can be hard travelling and a little bit tricky if you need to call on health specialists. So, I reluctantly had to pull out of the commentary job and sit tight until I got a sign that my health was on the mend and that I was strong enough to travel.

But it was a constant battle. I hated being ill and dependent on others. My self-confidence was low and I was really struggling. Sometimes I wouldn't, or couldn't, get out of bed. At times I wouldn't answer the phone. I don't know what I was afraid of – simple things were such a task. Jo was trying to pep me up and encourage me, but it was an awful period for us both. It just shows what sort of person she is to have survived that time with me. I can't praise her enough. Everything she stands for is good. And how lucky am I? Who knows what might've happened if she weren't there with me? I don't even like thinking about that possibility.

Fortunately Steve Norris also had faith in me. A month later I was asked to go to Pakistan to cover the Indian tour, and this time I was able to go. Jo came over for a couple of weeks, and everything went okay. I was heading in the right direction.

Around April and May my health began to improve, albeit ever so slightly. It was a case of two steps forward, one step back. I'd have a good day and be able to walk reasonably well, but then I'd get too excited and go out and do too much, and the next day would be very hard. Unfortunately, I wasn't improving quickly enough or getting anywhere close to being able to play yet – and the question of what I was going to do was nagging away at me. NSW Cricket had offered me a contract for the 2004/05 season, so I was caught in a serious dilemma. Should I sign it in the hope that by the start of the season I might be fit? Or maybe it was a completely unrealistic proposition. Was it time to face the reality that my playing days were over, and that this was my chance to leave the game on a good note? Was I going to have to retire and put my bat under the bed?

Coming to the conclusion that I was going to have to retire was almost as tough as dealing with my reactive arthritis. Each day I had a different viewpoint. I just didn't know what to do. But then one night I was up at Jo's parents' place at Palm Beach, way up in Sydney's northern beaches, sitting there watching TV by myself, when I had a moment of clarity. *You know what?* I thought. *I can't play anymore ... I'm hanging on to something that I just can't do. There's no way I can give my best.*

I would let both myself and my team-mates down. I'll end up struggling on for a couple of years trying to maintain a career that might peter out to nothing. And I certainly didn't want it to end that way. There was dignity in retiring and, realistically, it seemed that I had little choice given the state of my health. So the next day I made the phone calls, and five days later, on 9 June 2004, I was announcing my retirement.

It's funny, but when you're at your playing peak, you know that retirement's always out there in the distance somewhere, but you hope it's never going to happen. It seems so far away. So the day of my press conference was incredibly hard and full of heavy emotions for me. It was the most nervous I'd ever been in a public situation. It hurt to say: 'I'm here today to announce my retirement from first-class cricket ...' because you don't ever think you're going to say those words. Everyone could see that I was physically shaking; my voice was cracking up.

Fortunately, I was flanked by two good men, both full of support for me. On one side I had David Gilbert, chief executive of NSW Cricket, who'd always been incredibly supportive (and he was also the first bowler I faced in first-class cricket, oddly enough). On my right, I had Mark Taylor, my former opening partner and the NSW Cricket director. Mark said great things about me and what I'd done for the game. So as far as press conferences go, it was pretty good. Afterwards, I felt a great sense of relief. From then onwards it was all about getting my health right, both physically and mentally. And I realised that my negative mindset was very stressful for my relationship with Jo – so I had to work extra hard on that as well.

It was around that time that I returned to the Black Dog Institute in Randwick, which deals with depression. I'd already been there for an assessment months before to try to get to the bottom of my negative thoughts. My involvement with the organisation had come about through Neil Maxwell, who'd been managing me at the time. Neil had met the Black Dog's media guy in Canberra and my name had come up in relation to the hard time I'd had with the press. I then met up with him, with a view to taking on some kind of PR role: public speaking or representation, or something similar.

I had suffered some pretty low times in my life, mainly due to my AS and the pressure from the media, so I understood how awful it can be when you're down. And the fact is that young men suffer in silence most of the time when it comes to depression, so I thought it might be a good organisation to become involved with. Maybe there was something I could do to help out others. But although I was open to the idea, in the end I felt nervous about getting too deeply involved with an organisation that dealt with mental disorders. I thought it might prove to be more ammunition for the media. I also knew that I still wasn't on top of things personally and needed to do a lot more self-enquiry.

So at the end of that meeting with the media representative I decided to book myself in to see Professor Gordon Parker, for the first time, the following week. I was still struggling to find meaning, or sense, in a number of important aspects of my life, so I thought it might be a way to discover what was going on inside me. Professor Parker told me that, given the big things I'd been dealing with over a long time, my feelings of depression were perfectly natural. It was a good chat.

Black Dog also has a self-analysis program that you can work through, and when I visited the second time and completed it, Professor Parker looked over my answers and assessed me. He said that I might be a mild Bipolar II sufferer. This was a huge shock for me, being labelled as suffering from a fairly well-known mental condition.

To be honest, I'm not sure if Bipolar II fits the bill for me. There had been so many crazy things going on in my life for so long, that I think circumstantial depression seems more logical. And when you are categorised as Bipolar II, there needs to be an element of mania present. Looking back, I realise I probably had experienced some form of mania, but it had been due to the antidepressants I'd been incorrectly prescribed in the UK to treat my panic attacks. Yes, they'd taken away my anxiety, but they had elevated my mood. While I'd felt pretty normal at the time, and had a terrific season against the West Indies, I was probably experiencing some overexuberance, and I guess people saw that and commented on it.

But whether or not I had (or have) Bipolar II ... well, I'm not sure. Possibly I have experienced some symptoms that are characteristic of the condition, or maybe I just got so damn low because I had every reason to feel that way. I remember when Jo and I first got together, we spoke about being down and depressed. She expressed amazement at what I'd gone through, and told me that she would defy anyone to go through the same experiences and not get depressed.

● ⑬ ●

Following my retirement from playing cricket, there was no way I was going to sit idle for too long and wallow in self-pity. In fact, I was excited about the possibilities of the future, and in my heart I knew that commentary was something I wanted to pursue further. And I felt free. I experienced a real sense of liberation – no longer would my life be dictated by the regimen of a first-class cricketer. I was ready to move on to the next stage of my life.

A couple of offers to commentate soon rolled in and before long I was in Sri Lanka covering the Asia Cup for ESPN, then in Amsterdam for a triangular series, in the UK for the ICC Trophy, then in India for the much-anticipated Border-Gavaskar Trophy. During 2005, I've covered the Australian tour of New Zealand in March, and Pakistan's tour to the West Indies. And I've also been on the celebrated Ashes tour. What little time is left between tours I fill up with corporate appearances and speaking gigs. My life is incredibly rich again and I'm enjoying every day.

As a commentator, I'm hoping one day to score that dream job in the Channel 9 team, alongside my mates Mark Taylor and Ian Healy. I think it's around the corner; the way I see it, I'm now serving a good apprenticeship. It's a very different skill to articulate – rather than play – the game, but that's what stimulates me. And I think there are parallels between the way I played and the way I call the game. I really try to bring my emotions and energy into my commentary. As mentioned previously, Test cricket in particular is full of ebbs and flows, and I see my role as trying to get the viewer to feel and experience the game on a deeper level. There are a lot of extremely educated cricket viewers out there, so as a former Test cricketer I try to give them something extra to think about, drawing from my time in the heat of the battle.

Something I really enjoy at the moment is that I'm not too far removed from the game as a player. Hopefully, I can make a person sitting at home sipping a beer feel what it's really like to face Shoaib Akhtar or Anil Kumble. I find the travel testing, because it's a more lonely existence than being on tour with your team-mates, so you have a lot of downtime to kill. But I've always got a good book, occasionally I bring my guitar, and my computer helps me to keep in touch. I also like to get into the gym as often as I can.

As for cricket, I might even turn up for a grade game or two in the future, if I have the time, although I think I've picked up a bat and swung a good air cover drive only a couple of times in the past twelve months. But if I feel right in my body and my heart, who knows? I'm now off all medication for my AS – I'm completely drug-free and I hope to stay that way for the rest of my life. I get a little soreness in my feet in the morning, but I can deal with that. Yoga and a healthy lifestyle have been a fantastic help.

I'm feeling really strong these days. I've got my head around the fact that I'm now retired, even though I've had flashes recently – especially while calling games in New Zealand and India – where I'd be looking at guys I used to run around with and thinking it could still be me. But they're only fleeting moments. The way I see it, you have your chapter in the game, and then the game keeps going. I was lucky. I had a twelve-year career and played 74 Test matches and was able to achieve many great highs. I was in an awesome team that won way more Tests than most. Wow, what an *amazing* time I had.

As a cricketer, I want to be remembered as someone who gave his all and enjoyed what he was doing. I've always seen the game as a form of entertainment, so hopefully I've been able to perform in an entertaining fashion. My attitude to batting was always this: I had a hunk of wood in my hand for one reason and one reason only, to score runs and attack the bowling whenever I could. I think for the most part I stayed true to this. I was a passionate player who, for better or worse, wore his heart right out there on his sleeve. People have said that I influenced the aggressive way the champion Australian side plays today, and if this is true, then that's the highest accolade of all. I played the game the only way I knew how: full on.

My memories of playing always bring a smile to my face. To be one of a lucky few to have played cricket for Australia, I feel both truly blessed and extremely honoured. Even though the last couple of years could've been better, in my mind I left the game on a high. And while I may have some regrets, I feel no bitterness whatso-ever. It has been one hell of a journey to this point and one I have cherished.

I'll Sleep When I'm Dead

I once believed that playing cricket was everything, but now at 35 years of age I realise that my life has just started. As Jon Bon Jovi has often whispered into my ear, 'I'll sleep when I'm dead.'

Career Statistics

Test batting statistics

1993 Ashes Series – England v Australia

match	venue	date	inns 1	inns 2	res
1st Test	Old Trafford, Manchester	3–7 June	58	27	W
2nd Test	Lord's, London	17–21 June	152	–	W
	(wins Man of the Match award)				
3rd Test	Trent Bridge, Nottingham	1–6 July	40	26	D
4th Test	Headingley, Leeds	22–26 July	67	–	W
5th Test	Edgbaston, Birmingham	5–9 Aug	22	8	W
6th Test	Kennington Oval, London	19–23 Aug	4	12	L

1993/94 Trans-Tasman Trophy – Australia v New Zealand

match	venue	date	inns 1	inns 2	res
1st Test	WACA, Perth	12–16 Nov	10	99	D
2nd Test	Bellerive Oval, Hobart	26–30 Nov	168	–	W
3rd Test	Woolloongabba, Brisbane	3–7 Dec	28	–	W

1993/94 3-Test series – Australia v South Africa

match	venue	date	inns 1	inns 2	res
1st Test	MCG, Melbourne	26–30 Dec	32	–	D
2nd Test	SCG, Sydney	2–6 Jan	92	1	L
3rd Test	Adelaide Oval, Adelaide	28 Jan–1 Feb	53	7	W

1993/94 3-Test series – South Africa v Australia

match	venue	date	inns 1	inns 2	res
1st Test	Wanderers, Johannesburg	4–8 Mar	26	41	L
2nd Test	Newlands, Cape Town	17–21 Mar	26	43*	W
	(passes 1000 Test runs milestone)				
3rd Test	Kingsmead, Durban	25–29 Mar	20	95	D

1994/95 3-Test series – Pakistan v Australia

match	venue	date	inns 1	inns 2	res
1st Test	National Stadium, Karachi	28 Sept–2 Oct	36	23	L
2nd Test	Rawalpindi Stadium, Rawalpindi	5–9 Oct	110	1	D
3rd Test	Gaddafi Stadium, Lahore	1–5 Nov	74	–	D

1994/95 Ashes Series – Australia v England

match	venue	date	inns 1	inns 2	res
1st Test	Woolloongabba, Brisbane	25–29 Nov	176	45	W
2nd Test	MCG, Melbourne	24–29 Dec	3	44	W
3rd Test	SCG, Sydney	1–5 Jan	11	103	D
4th Test	Adelaide Oval, Adelaide	26–30 Jan	67	5	L
5th Test	WACA, Perth	3–7 Feb	124	45	W
	(passes 2000 Test runs milestone)				

1994/95 Frank Worrell Trophy – West Indies v Australia

match	venue	date	inns 1	inns 2	res
1st Test	Kensington Oval, Bridgetown	31 Mar–2 Apr	18	20*	W
2nd Test	Antigua Rec. Ground, St John's	8–13 Apr	41	18	D
3rd Test	Queen's Park Oval, Port of Spain	21–23 Apr	0	15	L
4th Test	Sabina Park, Kingston	29 Apr–3 May	27	–	W

1995/96 3-Test series – Australia v Pakistan

match	venue	date	inns 1	inns 2	res
1st Test	Woolloongabba, Brisbane	9–4 Nov	42	–	W
2nd Test	Bellerive Oval, Hobart	17–21 Nov	0	73	W
3rd Test	SCG, Sydney	30 Nov–4 Dec	1	23	L

1995/96 3-Test series – Australia v Sri Lanka

match	venue	date	inns 1	inns 2	res
1st Test	WACA, Perth	8–12 Dec	219	–	W
	(wins Man of the Match award)				
2nd Test	MCG, Melbourne	26–30 Dec	62	13*	W
3rd Test	Adelaide Oval, Adelaide	25–29 Jan	0	15	W

1996/97 Border-Gavaskar Trophy – India v Australia

match	venue	date	inns 1	inns 2	res
Test	Feroz Shah Kotla, Delhi	10–13 Oct	44	0	L

1997/98 Border-Gavaskar Trophy – India v Australia

match	venue	date	inns 1	inns 2	res
1st Test	MA Chidambaram Stadium, Chennai	6–10 Mar	11	13	L
2nd Test	Edens Gardens, Kolkata	18–21 Mar	0	5	L
3rd Test	M Chinnaswamy Stadium, Bangalore	25–28 Mar	91	42	W

1998/99 3-Test series – Pakistan v Australia

match	venue	date	inns 1	inns 2	res
1st Test	Rawalpindi Stadium, Rawalpindi	1–5 Oct	108	–	W
2nd Test	Arbab Niaz Stadium, Peshawar	15–19 Oct	2	21	D
3rd Test	National Stadium, Karachi	22–26 Oct	96	11	D
	(passes 3000 Test runs milestone)				

Career Statistics

1998/99 Ashes Series – Australia v England

match	venue	date	inns 1	inns 2	res
1st Test	Woolloongabba, Brisbane	20–24 Nov	16	113	D
2nd Test	WACA, Perth	28–30 Nov	34	17	W
3rd Test	Adelaide Oval, Adelaide	11–15 Dec	17	103	W
4th Test	MCG, Melbourne	26–29 Dec	1	18	L
5th Test	SCG, Sydney	2–5 Jan	18	123	W

1998/99 Frank Worrell Trophy – West Indies v Australia

match	venue	date	inns 1	inns 2	res
1st Test	Queen's Park Oval, Port of Spain	5–8 Mar	23	106	W
2nd Test	Sabina Park, Kingston	13–16 Mar	22	0	L
3rd Test	Kensington Oval, Bridgetown	26–30 Mar	23	26	L
4th Test	Antigua Rec. Ground, St John's	3–7 Apr	33	44	W

1999/2000 3-Test series – Sri Lanka v Australia

match	venue	date	inns 1	inns 2	res
1st Test	Asgiriya Stadium, Kandy (*50th Test match*)	9–11 Sept	0	27	L
2nd Test	Galle International Stadium, Galle (*wins Man of the Match award*)	22–26 Sept	96	–	D
3rd Test	Sinhalese Sports Club, Colombo	30 Sept–4 Oct	59	–	D

1999/2000 Southern Cross Trophy – Zimbabwe v Australia

match	venue	date	inns 1	inns 2	res
Test	Harare Sports Club, Harare	14–17 Oct	4	0*	W

1999/2000 3-Test series – Australia v Pakistan

match	venue	date	inns 1	inns 2	res
1st Test	Woolloongabba, Brisbane (*passes 4000 Test runs milestone*) (*wins Man of the Match award*)	5–9 Nov	169	32*	W
2nd Test	Bellerive Oval, Hobart	18–22 Nov	97	27	W
3rd Test	WACA, Perth	26–28 Nov	0	–	W

1999/2000 Border-Gavaskar Trophy – Australia v India

match	venue	date	inns 1	inns 2	res
1st Test	Adelaide Oval, Adelaide	10–14 Dec	28	0	W
2nd Test	MCG, Melbourne	26–30 Dec	91	3	W
3rd Test	SCG, Sydney	2–4 Jan	1	–	W

1999/2000 Trans-Tasman Trophy – New Zealand v Australia

match	venue	date	inns 1	inns 2	res
1st Test	Eden Park, Auckland	11–15 Mar	5	6	W

2nd Test	Basil Reserve, Wellington	24–27 Mar	143	12	W
	(*wins Man of the Match award*)				
3rd Test	Westpac Trust Park, Hamilton	31 Mar–3 Apr	2	9	W

2000/01 Frank Worrell Trophy – Australia v West Indies

match	venue	date	inns 1	inns 2	res
1st Test	Woolloongabba, Brisbane	23–25 Nov	54	–	W
2nd Test	WACA, Perth	1–3 Dec	19	–	W
3rd Test	Adelaide Oval, Adelaide	15–19 Dec	83	1	W
4th Test	MCG, Melbourne	26–29 Dec	30	4	W
5th Test	SCG, Sydney	2–6 Jan	96	86*	W
	(*wins Man of the Match award*)				

2000/01 Border-Gavaskar Trophy – India v Australia

match	venue	date	inns 1	inns 2	res
1st Test	Wankhede Stadium, Mumbai	27 Feb–1 Mar	10	19*	W
	(*passes 5000 Test runs milestone*)				
2nd Test	Edens Gardens, Kolkata	11–15 Mar	42	43	L
3rd Test	MA Chidambaram Stadium, Chennai	18–22 Mar	4	48	L

2001 Ashes Series – England v Australia

match	venue	date	inns 1	inns 2	res
1st Test	Edgbaston, Birmingham	5–8 July	77	–	W
2nd Test	Lord's, London	19–22 July	25	4	W
3rd Test	Trent Bridge, Nottingham	2–4 Aug	15	12	W
4th Test	Headingley, Leeds	16–20 Aug	21	16	L

Test batting averages

series	M	inns	NO	runs	HS	100s	50s	ave
1993 v England	6	10	0	416	152	1	2	41.60
1993/94 v New Zealand	3	4	0	305	168	1	1	76.25
1993/94 v South Africa	3	5	0	185	92	0	2	37.00
1993/94 v South Africa	3	6	1	251	95	0	1	50.20
1994/95 v Pakistan	3	5	0	244	110	1	1	48.80
1994/95 v England	5	10	0	623	176	3	1	62.30
1994/95 v West Indies	4	7	1	139	41	0	0	23.16
1995/96 v Pakistan	3	5	0	139	73	0	1	27.80
1995/96 v Sri Lanka	3	5	1	309	219	1	1	77.25
1996/97 v India	1	2	0	44	44	0	0	22.00
1997/98 v India	3	6	0	162	91	0	1	27.00
1998/99 v Pakistan	3	5	0	238	108	1	1	47.60
1998/99 v England	5	10	0	460	123	3	0	46.00

Career Statistics

series	M	inns	NO	runs	HS	100s	50s	ave
1998/99 v West Indies	4	8	0	277	106	1	0	34.62
1999/2000 v Sri Lanka	3	4	0	182	96	0	2	45.50
1999/2000 v Zimbabwe	1	2	1	4	4	0	0	4.00
1999/2000 v Pakistan	3	5	1	325	169	1	1	81.25
1999/2000 v India	3	5	0	123	91	0	1	24.60
1999/2000 v New Zealand	3	6	0	177	143	1	0	29.50
2000/01 v West Indies	5	8	1	373	96	0	4	53.28
2000/01 v India	3	6	1	166	48	0	0	33.20
2001 v England	4	7	0	170	77	0	1	24.28
career	74	131	7	5312	219	14	21	42.83

International limited-overs batting statistics

1993/94 B&H World Series – Australia/New Zealand/South Africa

match	opponent	venue	date	runs	res
Match 1	South Africa	MCG, Melbourne	9 Dec	73	L
Match 3	New Zealand	Adelaide Oval, Adelaide	12 Dec	8	W
Match 4	South Africa	SCG, Sydney	14 Dec	73	W

1993/94 One-Day International tournament – South Africa v Australia

match	opponent	venue	date	runs	res
Match 4	South Africa	Kingsmead, Durban	24 Feb	1	L
Match 5	South Africa	Buffalo Park, East London	2 Apr	31	W
Match 6	South Africa	St George's Park, Port Elizabeth	4 Apr	16	L
Match 8	South Africa	Springbok Park, Bloemfontein	8 Apr	34	W

1993/94 Austral-Asia Cup – United Arab Emirates/Australia/ New Zealand/Pakistan/Sri Lanka

match	opponent	venue	date	runs	res
Match 2	Sri Lanka	Sharjah CA Stadium, Sharjah	14 Apr	15	W
Match 4	New Zealand	Sharjah CA Stadium, Sharjah	16 Apr	0	W

1994 Singer World Series – Sri Lanka/Australia/India/Pakistan

match	opponent	venue	date	runs	res
Match 2	Pakistan	Sinhalese Sports Club, Colombo	7 Sept	4	W
Match 3	India	R Premadasa Stadium, Khettarama	9 Sept	26	L
Match 5	India	P Saravanamuttu Stadium, Colombo	13 Sept	24	L

1994/95 Wills Triangular Series – Pakistan/Australia/South Africa

match	opponent	venue	date	runs	res
Match 1	South Africa	Gaddafi Stadium, Lahore	12 Oct	44	W
Match 2	Pakistan	Ibn-e-Qasim Bagh Stadium, Multan	14 Oct	0	W

Match 4	South Africa	Iqbal Stadium, Faisalabad	18 Oct	38	W
Match 6	Pakistan	Rawalpindi Stadium, Rawalpindi	22 Oct	4	L
Match 7	South Africa	Arbab Niaz Stadium, Peshawar	24 Oct	54	W
Series final	Pakistan	Gaddafi Stadium, Lahore	30 Oct	66	W

1994/95 B&H World Series – Australia/England/Zimbabwe

match	opponent	venue	date	runs	res
Match 1	Zimbabwe	WACA, Perth	2 Dec	18	W
Match 3	England	SCG, Sydney	6 Dec	50	W
Match 4	Zimbabwe	Bellerive Oval, Hobart	8 Dec	18	W
(Match 6	Australia A	Adelaide Oval, Adelaide	11 Dec	64	W)
Match 10	Australia A	Woolloongabba, Brisbane	8 Jan	9	W
Match 11	England	MCG, Melbourne	10 Jan	2	L
(1st final	Australia A	SCG, Sydney	15 Jan	92	W)
(2nd final	Australia A	MCG, Melbourne	17 Jan	56	W)

1994/95 One-Day International tournament – West Indies v Australia

match	opponent	venue	date	runs	res
Match 1	West Indies	Kensington Oval, Bridgetown	8 Mar	21	L
Match 2	West Indies	Queen's Park Oval, Port of Spain	11 Mar	55	W
Match 3	West Indies	Queen's Park Oval, Port of Spain	12 Mar	1	L
Match 4	West Indies	Arnos Vale, Kingstown	15 Mar	68	L
Match 5	West Indies	Bourda, Georgetown	16 Mar	41	L

1995/96 B&H World Series – Australia/Sri Lanka/West Indies

match	opponent	venue	date	runs	res
Match 2	West Indies	Adelaide Oval, Adelaide	17 Dec	32	W
Match 3	West Indies	MCG, Melbourne	19 Dec	2	W
Match 4	Sri Lanka	SCG, Sydney	21 Dec	10	W
Match 5	West Indies	SCG, Sydney	1 Jan	5	W
Match 8	West Indies	Woolloongabba, Brisbane	7 Jan	0	L
Match 9	Sri Lanka	MCG, Melbourne	9 Jan	2	L

1996 Singer World Series – Sri Lanka/Australia/India/Zimbabwe

match	opponent	venue	date	runs	res
Match 1	Zimbabwe	R Premadasa Stadium, Khettarama	26 Aug	50	W
Match 3	Sri Lanka	R Premadasa Stadium, Khettarama	30 Aug	9	L
Match 6	India	Sinhalese Sports Club, Colombo	6 Sept	29	W
Series final	Sri Lanka	R Premadasa Stadium, Khettarama	7 Sept	8	L

1996/97 Titan Cup – India/Australia/South Africa

match	opponent	venue	date	runs	res
Match 3	India	M Chinnaswamy Stadium, Bangalore	21 Oct	3	L
Match 8	South Africa	Nehru Stadium, Guhawati	1 Nov	53*	L
Match 9	India	Punjab CA Stadium, Mohali	3 Nov	52	L

Career Statistics

1997 Texaco Trophy – England v Australia

match	opponent	venue	date	runs	res
Match 1	England	Headingley, Leeds	22 May	17	L
Match 2	England	Kennington Oval, London	24 May	1	L

International limited-overs batting averages

series	M	runs	HS	100s	50s	ave
1993/94 B&H World Series	3	91	73	0	1	30.33
1993/94 v South Africa	4	82	34	0	0	20.50
1993/94 Austral-Asia Cup	2	15	15	0	0	7.50
1994 Singer World Series	3	54	26	0	0	18.00
1994/95 Wills Triangular Series	6	206	66	0	2	34.33
1994/95 B&H World Series	4	80	50	0	1	20.00
1994/95 v West Indies	5	186	68	0	2	37.20
1995/96 B&H World Series	6	51	32	0	0	8.50
1996 Singer World Series	4	96	50	0	1	24.00
1996/97 Titan Cup	3	108	53*	0	2	54.00
1997 Texaco Trophy	2	18	17	0	0	9.00
career	42	987	73	0	9	24.07

Domestic seasons (Sheffield Shield/Pura Cup) for NSW

season	M	I	NO	runs	HS	100s	50s	ave
1991/92	2	3	0	98	62	0	1	32.66
1992/93	9	17	1	1005	143	3	6	62.81
1993/94	4	8	0	277	107	1	1	34.62
1994/95	3	5	0	161	70	0	2	32.20
1995/96	5	10	1	415	100*	1	3	46.11
1996/97	10	19	0	703	102	1	5	37.00
1997/98	7	14	0	550	137	1	3	39.28
1998/99	3	6	0	179	113	1	0	29.83
1999/2000	4	8	0	194	59	0	1	24.25
2000/01	2	3	0	118	100	1	0	39.33
2001/02	7	13	1	314	58*	0	2	26.16
2002/03	10	18	0	770	204	3	1	42.77
2003/04	3	6	0	106	45	0	0	17.66
career	69	130	3	4890	204	12	25	38.50

Domestic limited-overs competitions (Mercantile Mutual Cup/ING Cup) for NSW by season

season	M	I	NO	runs	HS	100s	50s	ave
1992/93	2	2	0	58	54	0	1	29.00
1993/94	2	2	0	121	96	0	1	60.50
1994/95	0	0	–	–	–	–	–	–
1995/96	4	4	0	84	77	0	1	21.00
1996/97	3	3	0	33	14	0	0	11.00
1997/98	5	5	0	180	68	0	2	36.00
1998/99	4	4	0	60	33	0	0	15.00
1999/2000	5	5	0	96	45	0	0	19.20
2000/01	9	9	0	205	61	0	2	22.77
2001/02	5	5	0	73	35	0	0	14.60
2002/03	8	5	1	75	26	0	0	18.75
2003/04	3	3	1	38	27	0	0	19.00
career	50	47	2	1023	96	0	7	22.73

Index

Index